My Wonderful Amazing Beautiful Life

Vignettes in the life of a Foreign Services Officer of the U.S. State Department

by Maurice J. Hyder

My Wonderful Amazing Beautiful Life

Copyrights and Credits:

Title- My Wonderful Amazing Beautiful Life
Author - Maurice J. Hyder
My Wonderful Amazing Beautiful Life
Text copyright © 2015 Maurice Hyder
 Photographs of the Hyder Family taken by various sources.
 All domestic and international copyrights apply. All Copyright ©2015
 Evacuation of Viet Nam Photographs provided by Corbis Media.
 All other Photographs copyright Maurice Hyder.
 All Rights Reserved.

 No part of this publication may be reproduced, stored in a retrieval system, transmitted in any form, or by any form, electronic, mechanical, photocopying, recording, or otherwise, without the written permission of the Publisher.

 ISBN(13) 978-158478-053-3
 ISBN (10)   1-58478-053-3
 Library of Congress Control Number: 2015912473
 Highlands Press, Paradise, California

Vignettes in the life of a foreign services officer of the United States State Department.
 BISAC - History/ World/ General
Printed in the United States of America /
First Edition   First Printing 2015

DEDICATION

This book is dedicated to the wonderful woman who shared my life, Sheila Howard Hyder. She was a blind date arranged by her friends at a graduation party in 1956 at the American University in Beirut, Lebanon.

Sheila shared the difficult path I had committed myself to in carrying out the mission placed on me by the United States State Department. Sheila is the author of a published book on children's stories that is available on the Internet at amazon.com.

-Table of Contents-

Chapter One	Born in Springfield	1
Chapter Two	My Boy Scout Adventure	7
Chapter Three	The Sea Scouts	15
Chapter Four	Into the Navy	21
Chapter Five	Out to Sea and Errol Flynn	37
Chapter Six	Baskinta	51
Chapter Seven	The New FSO	59
Chapter Eight	Sheila	67
Chapter Nine	Our Wedding	81
Chapter Ten	Our First Born and the Crown Prince	89
Chapter Eleven	The Supply Officer	97
Chapter Twelve	Baby Chicks	109
Chapter Thirteen	Off to Viet Nam	119
Chapter Fourteen	Back Stateside	127
Chapter Fifteen	Ipanema Beach and the Boy Scouts	133
Life Gallery		139
Chapter Sixteen	One Ton of Beer	167
Chapter Seventeen	The Phillipines	177
Chapter Eighteen	The Viet Nam Evacuation	197

Chapter Nineteen	*The Hospital*	*203*
Chapter Twenty	*Mi No Wuk II*	*207*
Chapter Twenty One	*The Boy Scouts of America*	*221*
Chapter Twenty Two	*The Departure*	*233*
Chapter Twenty Three	*Sheila's Message*	*237*
Epilogue		*241*
Vital Statistics		*245*
Acknowledgements		*247*

Chapter 1

Born in Springfield

Chapter 1 Born in Springfield

I was born to Lebanese parents in Springfield, Massachusetts 30 April 1922 and had three brothers: Theodore, Frederick, and Richard. My father, Charles N. Hyder, was laid off in 1924 as a master machinist six years after the end of World War I. My mother, Adele Malouf Hyder, was an accomplished concert pianist and had received a Bachelor of Arts at Wellesley College.

My ancestors originated from southwestern Syria in the area called the Houreen which was part of Canaan. Many of the Christian tribes of that area immigrated for religious reasons to the high mountains of Lebanon for their protection around the 14th century. The Abouhaider settled in a village called Baskinta at an elevation of more than 5,000 feet on Mt. Sannine. All of the area of the Middle East at that time was part of the Ottoman Empire. It was a standard procedure for the Ottoman Empire to take young Christian boys 7-8 years old to Ottokan Training Camps in Turkey. These boys were formed into military units called Janissaries to fight for the Sultan of the Ottoman Empire. Toward the end of the 19th century my father's mother, Hundoumeh Abouhaider who was the sister of the Priest at the Eastern Orthodox Church at Springfield, Massachusetts decided to bring her children to the United States so that her sons would escape the Ottoman Janissary military draft.

In 1895 she secretly collected her three sons and daughter with money she had saved. Then, made arrangements with a Greek ship captain at Beirut, Lebanon to take her and children to France.

With the help of the Greek captain they were able to arrange onward passage to the United States and entered through the port of Boston and New York. My paternal grandmother, with the help of her brother, Father Moses Abouhaider of the E. Orthodox Church, the family was relocated to Springfield, Massachusetts. When my grandmother, accompanied by my father Charles and his brothers Abdullah, Wilfred, and daughter Nellie, were entered on the emigration records their last names were abbreviated from Abouhaider to Hyder. My father had been educated in Lebanon at an orthodox seminary to become a priest but my grandmother urged him to change his mind saying "Priests don't make money and he should learn a trade to get a good job." The children went to school in Massachusetts. My father attended a trade school at night and became a machinist. As the war in Europe escalated, my father was hired in 1910 by the U.S. Armory at Springfield, Massachusetts making guns and other hardware for the military and upcoming war.

He was laid off in 1924 as a master machinist six years after the end of World War I. My mother, Adele Malouf Hyder, was an accomplished concert pianist and had

Chapter 1 Born in Springfield

received a Bachelor of Arts at Wellesley College.

My maternal grandmother, Ghalia Sliman Maalouf Hyder, and grandfather, Monsieur Joseph Hyder, also from Lebanon, owned a thriving import company on Main Street in Springfield, Massachusetts. It was known as the M.J.Hyder Importing Company, specializing in oriental rugs, imported handmade linens and furniture. By 1920, my grandmother owned the five story building in which her company maintained the showroom on the first floor. She also acquired an office building next door in which there was a theatre. She was well-known throughout New England and her customers were among the wealthy people between Boston and New York. She owned a beautiful five story tapestry brick home on three acres of land in West Springfield. One of her closest friends was Mrs. Calvin Coolidge, wife of President Calvin Coolidge.

I remember the nurse that my mother had employed who would take me in a pram across to walk in beautiful Van Horn Park. One day the nurse, Ann, took me across to the park. It seemed to me that she had a male friend who visited her when I was in the park and I was surprised at how they acted toward each other. When Ann returned me home that day, I told my mother that the strange man was biting Ann on the face. Mother laughed when she picked me up and told me he was not biting Ann but giving her a kiss.

In 1929, the financial world hit bottom affecting a large majority of people who lost their savings and had difficulty staying financially afloat. My Grandfather, M. J. Hyder had been a playboy and had a mistress and lost considerable amounts of money at gambling and betting on horses. My grandmother scraped any money she could gather selling her assets and thought she was able to break even when she was confronted by three men in black hats and dark suits who presented her with IOUs totaling more than $90,000. These were gambling debts generated by her husband. This was the end for her. She could not pay those bills and was forced into bankruptcy. She divorced my grandfather for putting her into jeopardy and still having his mistress. The judge who heard her case told her the home she owned and other assets would be sold to help pay the creditors. He told her she could take as much out of her home that would fit into a 5-ton truck. My mother's grand piano could not fit into that truck. and was strapped to the back of it. In 1929, during the drive from Springfield to Ansonia, Connecticut, the straps holding the grand piano broke and the piano dropped into the road and was destroyed.

My mother was so heartbroken, it was many years before she touched a piano again.

Chapter 1 Born in Springfield

Chapter Two
My Boy Scout Adventure

CHAPTER TWO MY BOY SCOUT ADVENTURE

When I lived in Ansonia, Connecticut on the Naugatuck River, if you walked half a mile out of town you were in dense woods. I had been reading the book The Last of the Mohicans by Fennimore Cooper. I was so caught up with the early history of our country. I dreamed that I had been reborn as an American Indian.

I had two friends, Eddie and Pete Musante, who lived nearby who would go hiking into the woods with me. We used our imagination and made our own bow and arrows, going into the deep woods hoping to kill a deer. We saw one; we shot our arrows but never came close. We would also bike to the South of Ansonia to the Housatonic River. We had better luck fishing than we had while hunting. Our families were happy to receive the fish we brought home.

Early in 1932, my father received a letter from the United States government asking him to go to Newport, Rhode Island to work at the United States Naval Torpedo

Station, making torpedoes for American submarines.

He was a skilled machinist and became a supervisor. He then located a home on Bliss Road in Newport, bought a car, and picked us up from Ansonia, Connecticut taking our family to Newport, Rhode Island.

There I joined the Boy Scouts of America. With my emphasis on outdoor living, I rapidly moved up the Boy Scout ladder. By June 1934, I became a Life Scout with more than 10 merit badges. I was a member of Troop 13 at the Second Baptist Church in Newport.

I was a member of the Pioneer Patrol and was elected by my fellow scouts as their patrol leader. I thrived on the scouting challenges presented before me. By 1936, I had 26 merit badges including all of the badges required for the Eagle Scout rank. I attended a Narragansett Council jamboree in Providence, Rhode Island, I took first place in the fire building contest using flint and steel, receiving an award from the hands of Daniel Beard an icon of the Boy Scout movement. Early in July 1937, I again attended summer at Camp Yawgoog in eastern Rhode Island where I was inducted into the Winneshiek Indians which was the forerunner of the Order of the Arrow Honor Camping Society.

In 1937, my brothers Ted, Fred, and I attended the first American World Boy Scout Jamboree that was held in Washington, D.C. The sight of that jamboree was on the beautiful grounds between the Lincoln Memorial and the United States Capitol. At that jamboree I was very excited when I was one of the scouts that met and shook hands with Baden Powell from England, the founder of the world scouting movement.

Chapter Two My Boy Scout Adventure

At age 14, I was a senior scout and was trained to do community service in Newport whenever an emergency occurred. We were trained as messengers, traffic directors, assisting firemen and providing first aid when needed. We took this responsibility seriously. All senior Boy Scouts in the Newport District had mobilization assignments during emergencies. As I had mentioned previously, I loved the challenges, and one evening in September 1938 after a troop meeting, members of my patrol and I were sitting in Touro Park, shooting the breeze.

We looked up at a statue on a pedestal in the center of Touro Park about 30 feet away from where we were sitting. The statue was of Oliver Hazard Perry, who was born in Newport and considered the hero of the Battle of Lake Erie. We got up, walked around the statue, and speculated noticing Oliver Howard Perry's extended arm was pointing towards the west depicting the words on the brass plaque at the bottom of the statue, stating his words We Have Met the Enemy, And They Are Ours. Laughing wouldn't it be funny to put a lantern on the end of the finger which was about 18 feet above the ground. My buddy said we couldn't do it. After I looked it over I made a bet that I could. I noticed a red lantern on a sidewalk repair area.

My friends asked: "How are you going to get up there?"

I replied, "Watch me!" On reviewing my challenge I noticed a bronzed two inch thick rope coiled at the bottom of the statue's feet on top of the pedestal. "One of you will cross the street and borrow a clothes line pole and bring it back to me." I was wearing ankle high sneakers and walked about 25 paces away. I turned and ran back as fast as I could up the pedestal. When reaching the apex of my run, I reached with my right hand and grabbed the bronze rope and pulled myself up to the top of the pedestal. One of my buddies brought me the clothes line pole which had an indentation at the end and handed it up to me. I held the tip down to them and they hooked the lantern on the pole. I carefully swung the pole out to the end of the finger of the statue and hooked the illuminated lantern on the finger, then jumped down. My buddies found a piece of cloth and a McCall's magazine and put the cloth around the shoulders of a Grecian muse shoulders, and put the magazine in her arms. We went back to our original bench and admired our efforts; the clothes line pole was returned to where it had been borrowed. This occurred about 7:00 p.m.

We noticed some automobile traffic coming down Broadway to circle the park and were beginning to stop. We were told later they thought there was a new stop light and stopped accordingly. Unsuccessfully, the Newport Police saw the problem and attempted to get the lantern down. They called the Fire Department for assistance and had to remove a section of an iron perimeter fence to permit a fire ladder truck to come into the park. At the same time there were movie theatres on each side of the park and people were coming out and having a great fun teasing the Police and Fire Departments who were trying to get the lamp down. Their effort almost toppled the statue. This only added to the enjoyment of the bystanders!

The Police Department started an investigation to find the culprits who created this incident. A member of the

Chapter Two My Boy Scout Adventure

Associated Press who was currently at Newport wrote an article about the incident that suggested Oliver Hazard Perry, being an old salt, was taking the opportunity to warn the Newport populist that a major storm was approaching from the northeast and to be prepared. A few weeks later the great disastrous hurricane of 1938 occurred, destroying more than 500 homes, and wiping out all the structures at Newport Beach.

A couple of months went by and we thought we were home free but one of the boys had told his girlfriend who was involved in the incident.

In November my father's cousin, Sgt. George Hyder in the Newport Police Department came to my home and my mother if I was home that he would like to talk to me. My mother called me and said George was outside and wanted to ask me some questions. I went down to his car and he asked me to sit down for a few minutes. He said the police had received rumors that I was one of the persons in the statue incident and asked me if the rumors were true. I told him the truth. He said I had to go with him to the police station to talk to the Chief of Police. When I arrived there, two members of my patrol who helped me during the incident, Ed Sherman and Bill Ibscher, were already there. They whispered to me, "What do we do?" and I said, "Tell the truth." The Chief and other members of his department interviewed us separately, and then put us together in a conference room.

The Chief said, "All of your stories support each other but we find it hard to believe that it could be done the way it was described." The Chief asked if I would reenact the incident. I agreed to do so and performed the stunt again much to the amazement of the police and Fire Department. We were returned to the police station where we received a lecture and were released to our parents. Following the Associated Press articles, many newspapers carried the story of Oliver Hazard Perry's warning the people of Newport of the approaching 1938 hurricane which occurred after the incident. I will never forget the incident.

Chapter Two My Boy Scout Adventure

Chapter Three
The Sea Scouts

CHAPTER THREE THE SEA SCOUTS

By March 1938, I had completed all of the merit badges required for the Eagle Rank plus 10 more miscellaneous badges. I had also completed my service project and was waiting for the next Court of Honor which was scheduled for November of 1938 to receive my Eagle badge. My Scoutmaster of Troop 13 was Eno Dahlquist. Among some of the new merit badges were seamanship, navigating, piloting, star study, sailing, and small boat handling. I also was the Boson of the Sea Scout ship. With the help of an old whaling ship captain our Sea Scout unit was becoming very popular. The District Commissioner helped us register a new Sea Scout ship in the Newport district. With the help of the Admiral at the Newport Naval Training Station, we were given permission to hold our Sea Scout meetings aboard the USS Constellation, the sister ship of Old Iron Sides of the War of 1812.

The USS Constellation was permanently moored at

the U.S. Naval Training Station at Newport. Our ship's skipper trained us weekly to row the Constellation long boat.

In May 1939, members of our Sea Scouts, including me, joined the 9th Division at the Naval Reserve in Newport. At our first meeting in June, the Admiral from the training station visited us aboard the Constellation. He told us that he had been observing our progress in rowing the long boat. He asked us if we would accept a challenge from the training recruits at the Naval Training Station for a two-mile rowing contest. He told them if they could beat the Sea Scouts, he would give them overnight liberty. The U.S. Navy Recruits were sure they could beat the youngest Sea Scouts and they had a shoe-in for liberty. Our Sea Scout ship captain said he thought we were ready and we accepted the challenge.

The next Saturday was the date of the race which was to start at 10:00 a.m. We were ready at the starting point when the Naval Training boat and crew arrived. The Admiral was there in his gig and said he would fire a shot in the air to start the race. Our skipper told us to keep our eyes on him and he would control the rhythm of the rowing. He said we would start with 10 hard short strokes to get the boat moving; then we would follow the stroke oar with smooth long strokes. The average weight of the Sea Scouts was 145 pounds while the average weight of the naval recruits was 185. After the Admiral shot the gun and started the race, the Navy recruits got off to a faster start and were about 5 lengths ahead of us. The course was 2 miles long. The Sea Scouts slowly caught up with the Navy recruits at the end of the first mile

Chapter Three The Sea Scouts

and forged ahead to cross the finish line 6 lengths ahead of the Navy recruits.

A week later the Admiral again attended a meeting aboard the Constellation and told us that he was so proud that he wanted to do something for us. He said he wanted to make available to us a World War I seventy-five (75) foot patrol boat for the use of the Sea Scouts. He asked us what we thought of the idea. One of the fellows asked, "Can we take it fishing and can we have our girlfriends join us?" He said yes! He told us that he would assign a United States Navy Officer to command the boat.

We made many local trips to Block Island, Martha's Vineyard, Montauk Point, and fishing for blue fish off Gardeners Island.

In mid-July a group of Naval Reserves from the 9th Division, United States Navy, including my buddies and myself, were sent to Norfolk, Virginia for our annual two week Naval Reserve training. During the first week we were taught to identify naval vessels by silhouette within two seconds, i.e., submarines, destroyers, cruisers, battleships, and aircraft carriers. Our training ship was a destroyer, the DD-108, USS Williams.

While underway the middle of the first week I was assigned to be the lookout as the weather was foggy off the Virginia coast. I was sent up to the lookout pulpit on the main mast. During that assignment I kept a careful watch in all directions and noticed a dark shape ahead of us. While keeping my eyes on the dark object in the distance, a partial bit of the fog lifted and I identified it as an aircraft carrier. I crawled down to the bridge and told the Officer of the Deck (OOD) that an aircraft carrier was dead ahead of us. He asked questions about what I was seeing and the direction it was traveling. I reported that it looked like the USS Lexington and was traveling from our port to starboard and suggested that we make a turn to port of 90° in order to stay clear of the vessel ahead. Fifteen (15) minutes later we could see the Lexington clearly about two hundred (200) yards ahead, passing to our starboard.

A week later 6 of our group was transferred to a minesweeper for training in minesweeping. Because this was a temporary assignment the USS Williams provided the 6 of us with a bag lunch. Since I was a Quartermaster Striker, I became the helmsman on the minesweeper. Ed Sherman who was on the wing of the bridge as a lookout ran to me, very excited, and said the OOD had fainted and was vomiting. In the meantime another of the reserves who was on deck had rushed to the bridge saying that all the members of the crew had passed out on the deck and was vomiting green substance. I told Sherman to take the wheel and stay steady on the course we were traveling. I ran into the wing of the bridge grabbing the semaphore flags stored there and quickly signaled to the USS Williams that we had an emergency on board with a short description and requested immediate assistance. They signaled back to me that they were sending over a line to connect a breech buoy and would be transferring an officer, a medical corpsman, and one engineer.

I reflected that again my Boy Scout training and my skills with signaling had been helpful. The officer came aboard and directed the removal of all connecting lines. The medical corpsman identified that the officers and

CHAPTER THREE THE SEA SCOUTS

crew of the minesweeper were suffering from ptomaine poisoning.

Upon researching the cause it was determined that the cook on the minesweeper had used porcelain covered iron bowl and aluminum spoon.

That bowl was damaged in many places exposing the metal causing contamination to the salad. We immediately followed the USS Williams back to Norfolk at Flank Speed. I received a written commendation from the Navy for the actions I had taken.

In July 1939, we took our patrol boat down to the site of the 1939 World Fair at the western point of Long Island Sound.

We had 3 glorious days at the fair and then returned home.

Chapter Four
Into the Navy

Chapter Four Into the Navy

We were all back in school in September.

Ed Sherman, Bill Ibascher, and I were seniors and in the class of 1940. In mid-October 1939, I returned home from school and my mother told me there was an official looking letter marked URGENT on the hall table. I opened it up and it stated that

"UPON RECEIPT OF THESE ORDERS YOU WILL REPORT WITHIN 24 HOURS TO THE COMMANDANT, FIRST NAVAL DISTRICT, BOSTON, MASSACHUSETTS."

My mother said that couldn't be correct and that I was a senior student at Rogers High School and hadn't yet graduated. Within the hour a moving police cruiser with loud speakers was announcing that all students from Rogers High School who received mobilization orders were to report to the high school auditorium at 5:00 p.m. that evening with our parents.

Our Rhode Island Congressman addressed all of the parents and students at the high school auditorium that President Roosevelt had placed the United States in a State of National Emergency and that he had placed all military reserves on active duty. My brother Ted Hyder was a member of the Rhode Island National Guard assigned to Fort Adams and had also received activation orders a few days later. He was present at the Battle of Guadalcanal, and had received a bullet wound in his right leg. He received a Purple Heart, but had survived the war. We had to carry out the orders accordingly. All military personnel were to report to the high school at 8:00 a.m. where the buses would be provided and would take us to our assignments.

Upon arrival at the First Naval District of Boston, we were sent to the Commonwealth Pier #1 at East Boston, which was the Mine Warfare Center. We were trained aboard the minesweeper in planting mines at all ports down the East Coast of the United States in water and also retrieving the minds. In 1940, we went to sea aboard the World War I destroyers, Eagle 19 and Eagle 27, on neutrality patrol in the North Atlantic.

In January 1941, we saw a Notice from the United States Navy Department requesting volunteers for The Armed Guard. No one seemed to know anything about the Armed Guard. My buddies and I volunteered for it since it seemed a better service than working with the mines; little did we know we were jumping from the frying pan into the fire! We started training on the Eagle ships learning the maintenance and firing of the four inch 50 cannon and machine guns.

Chapter Four Into the Navy

In May I was awarded the rank of Third Class Gunner's Mate and became gun captain of a 10-man gunnery crew.

In June the ships delivered us to an area off the north coast of Virginia called Little Creek. We were put ashore and found only corn stalks. We were met by a company of Marines that helped us clear out the area and put up tents in which to live.

We continued training with five inch, four inch, three inch, 20-mm and other machine guns in the Atlantic off the coast of Virginia. We were not permitted to take any liberty.

We were told that the Armed Guard as a military organization was illegal when the United States was not yet in a state of war. We all had to sign a top secret document and were told not to discuss the name of our group or the purpose for which we were organized.

In September we were all transported to the new Armed Guard Base at First Avenue and 52nd Street in Brooklyn, New York, called the Armed Guard Center. Again we asked for liberty and it was denied. Marine guards were posted to restrict our movements and make sure that there was no communication outside the Armed Guard Armory.

In mid-November, the entire Armed Guard crews sat down on the floor in the Armory, not saying a word. The Commander of the Armed Guard, Lieutenant Commander (Lt. Com.), United States Navy, William Coakley, came out on his bridge which was a veranda on the second deck. He called down to us that we had duty assignments and we should be working and our actions could be construed as Mutiny. He said we could be put in the brig and asked what was wrong with us.

Maurice Hyder U.S. Navy

Chapter Four Into the Navy

All the Armed Guard crew started to speak in a low voice but loud enough for the Commander to hear. "WE WANT LIBERTY TO GO HOME TO OUR FAMILIES FOR THANKSGIVING!" He told us that we had all signed a top secret document which included that no liberty was permitted. He went back into his office and made a telephone call. Five minutes later he returned to address us and said our request was being considered by the Navy Department. We then returned to our duties.

The next morning we were told that permission had been granted subject to the top secret document we had signed and that could not discuss in any way what we were doing in Brooklyn or our assignment in the Armed Guard. We were given a one week leave to visit our families for Thanksgiving.

On Sunday, 7 December, we were shocked to hear of the Japanese sneak attack on Pearl Harbor.

President Roosevelt was very concerned that the next target of the Japanese would be to attack the Panama Canal. He ordered that the United States Marines be deployed immediately to protect the Canal. They were to be transported to the Canal on the SS Exeter.

On Monday at 0600 8 December, we received orders to report to the United States Navy yard, Brooklyn and board the SS Exeter as the assigned United States Navy gun crew We carried only small arms. It should be noted here that the Exeter had not as yet received its required protective armament. A battalion of Marines came aboard the Exeter at 0700 and at 0800. Our ship got underway and proceeded south directly to the Panama Canal at Flank Speed.

My men and I had or own rifles and I carried a 35 caliber pistol. Our immediate duties were to ensure that the ship had total blackout. We were to restrict internal ship movement during the voyage of Marines from their assigned spaces until we arrived at the Canal. Upon arrival the Marines were disembarked and deployed to protect the Canal.

A few days later we arrived at Tampa, Florida. Within an hour, after Exeter was tied up to the pier, the Captain called me to the bridge. He showed me a new cable he had just received which stated: "Upon receipt of this cable you will turn over command of your vessel to the Senior Naval Person present. The Captain and his crew will depart on Exeter as soon as possible. Hyder that would be you. I give you here with the keys to all the spaces aboard the ship and turn over the Captain's quarters to you." He showed me where the keys to all of the ships' departments were kept, and then saluted me. I saluted him. The Captain and his crew had departed the ship within 30 minutes.

I posted guards on the pier at the bow and stern of the ship and main gangway. I told my men to be packed and ready to go ashore with minimum notice. My crew obtained food from the ship's freezer, i.e., ham, ice cream, and so on. I slept in the Captain's cabin to be close to the gangway.

The next morning about 9:00 a.m. the gangway watch called me and said, "Cars were arriving on the pier and Senior Naval Officers were heading for the gangway." I ordered all hands to the rail and salute upon my order. The senior Admiral arrived at the gangway, made a half turn and saluted the colors on the stern of the ship, then

Chapter Four Into the Navy

faced me, and said, "Gunner Mate Hyder, you are relived." I saluted him and said, "I stand relieved, Sir."

With all due respect I was so surprised at what had just happened. I realized that a Third Class Gunner's Mate had been relieved by a Vice Admiral and burst out laughing.

The next Admiral in line said, "HYDER, SHOW A LITTLE RESPECT!" I apologized for my outburst as the reality of what just took place in that Gunner's Mate Hyder was replaced by a Vice Admiral. The Admiral accepted my apology while the rest of the officers on the gangway were smiling. The Admiral told me to take my crew ashore and board the bus that was just arriving.

He said, "You will be transported to your next command at Mobile, Alabama." My new command was aboard the SS Edward Luckenbach. This ship had already received the approved armament. There was a five-inch 51-mm cannon from World War I mounted on the stern gun platform and four 50 caliber machine guns, two at the bow, and two on the bridge. My main five-inch gun was rusty and we set to work getting it cleaned up, repainted, completely serviceable with all working parts and firing mechanisms in good working order.

I asked the naval officer at Mobile, Alabama where I could obtain some U.S. Navy gray paint. He said, "None was available; the only color I could get was baby blue." My big gun barrel was very pretty in its new color. We had no ammunition for our guns. We left Mobile a week later on 18 December and headed south, passed through the Panama Canal into the Pacific and headed north. We took on fuel at the Port of San Pedro, California, and the Port of Los Angeles. Again we headed north to the ammunition depot at Antioch, California. The Luckenbach was one of the largest freighters afloat with eight hatches. They loaded gun powder and shells for our 5-inch guns and ammunition for our machine guns. Munitions of all types filled the forward four hatches. After loading was completed we left Antioch and proceeded to the Portland, Oregon Ammunition Depot where we filled our remaining after hatches with ammunitions and bombs. We then left Portland heading west without any escort.

My men, including me, were all scared. We were nothing more than a big floating bomb with all the explosives aboard. Two days later we arrived at Pearl Harbor and observed four Navy ships were still burning from the sneak attack. We topped off our fuel bunkers and left the next day, heading west alone.

The Captain opened his orders a few hours after we were at sea which identified our destination as Melbourne, Australia. We had instructions such as "zig zag" as necessary. The next day at sea we fire tested all guns and found them in good working order and ready for the defense of the vessel. We maintained lookouts 2 on the bow and 2 on the stern throughout the voyage except at night when my crew and some of the merchant men joined us around the big gun and said prayers including the Lord's Prayer for a safe passage to Australia. We repeated this procedure every night until we reached Melbourne. With God's blessing we made it. We did see 2 ships on the horizon during our passage. While at Melbourne the Australian military off loaded our vessel and said that much of the munitions were being sent to General Montgomery in North Africa.

Chapter Four Into the Navy

We left Melbourne ten days later and went to Hobart, Tasmania and took on wool in hatches 1 and 2. We then went to Auckland and Wellington, New Zealand and took on wool in hatches 3 and 4.

We enjoyed our liberty in New Zealand. We then left New Zealand and headed east toward South America. We arrived at the Port of Antofagasta, Chile where we took on a cargo for hatches 5 and 6 of potassium nitrate and into hatches 7 and 8 of manganese dioxide. When these 2 minerals are combined they are used to make gun powder and explosives.

After Chile we went north, stopped at the Port of Mollendo, Peru. It was not a typical port with a bay and piers; ships dropped anchors close to the coast since the water was very deep at that point. It was the most interesting situation to try to go ashore. The water went right up to the cliff wall which was approximately 60 feet high. A derrick was at the top of the cliff with a large wooden chair about 4 feet x 6 feet that was lowered down to just above the boat. The chair, when in use, could carry ten or more passengers, all clinging onto the chair. Mollendo was a very pretty and interesting town. I purchased a number of silver items for gifts for my family back home.

I tried my Spanish in negotiating in the items I desired. The young sales person looked up at me and said, "Would you prefer to use English. I'm a graduate of the University of San Diego." To say that we were startled was an understatement. My men and I enjoyed our discussions with her. We were told there were large silver mines nearby. Silver was a major export from that area.

We left 3 days later and went north and east through

the Panama Canal to the Gulf of Mexico. We stopped at the east end of the Canal for some minor repairs to the ship and then headed north to our next destination, New Orleans, Louisiana. While enroute we observed more than four ships burning and sinking as we headed towards Key West.

Two days later we passed Key West which was on the southern tip of Florida at about 4:00 p.m. Two hours later our ship suffered three major explosions sinking our ship. The Captain gave the order to abandon ship. My gun crew stayed aboard for another 15 minutes manning our guns in case an enemy surfaced and might endanger our life boats.

The merchant crews were able to get 2 lifeboats into the water. The rafts which should have been able to drop in the water with a quick release mechanism, didn't work. My men and I jumped into the water and swam to the lifeboats that were about 100 yards from the Luckenbach. I was the last person to reach the lifeboats and all I wore was a pair of basketball shorts. The boat was already overloaded with merchant men and some of my crew.

Every time I reflect on the incident I can smell and taste the ship's bunker fuel that was spilling out from the hull of the Luckenbach. A member of my crew in the lifeboat tied a rope around my hand to make sure I wouldn't drift away from the lifeboat. My greatest fear was of a possible shark attack and every time I felt water ripples near my body I looked for a shark fin.

The Captain had a flair gun pistol and fired 3 emergency flairs into the sky to alert the Navy Base at Key West of our predicament. After more than 30 hours

Chapter Four Into the Navy

in the water, four commercial fishing boats came out and picked us up and took us to Key West. We asked, "What took so long?" They said they didn't want to take the chance in case some enemy submarines were present. We were given temporary clothing by the Red Cross and a warm meal. We were then taken to Palm Beach, put on a train, and went to Brooklyn, to the Armed Guard Center where we were debriefed about the sinking incident. At this time I was promoted to Second Class Gunners Mate. We received our back pay, a new sea bag of clothing and given 15 days for survivor leave.

Sherman, Ibscher, and I went to Newport, Rhode Island to be with our families. While we were in Newport we were interviewed by the local newspaper and told our story of the sinking of our ship and our survival. We enjoyed that short opportunity to visit with our families, and after a week and a half, returned to the Armed Guard Center for reassignment. A new group of men were assigned to be my next gun crew. Sherman and Ibscher became new gun Captains with men assigned to them and were sent to other ships. With the crew assigned to me, we boarded a new Liberty ship and started out from New York to join a convoy in the Atlantic. After passing out to sea approximately 50 miles east from the Statue of Liberty my ship was torpedoed and sank very quickly. We were picked up by nearby vessels and were returned to the Armed Guard Center in Brooklyn.

I received a new and much larger gun crew and was assigned to the MV Saturnia, an Italian luxury passenger ship, which had arrived at the Port of New York. It had been escorted by United States Coast Guard vessels.

The ship was boarded by members of the Coast Guard and the F.B.I. The Captain and his entire crew had surrendered to the American authorities and gave their Parole to abide by an agreement that they were required to sign. They agreed to do so. The Captain and crew of this ship had defected to America and would turn over the ship to the United States, Merchant Marine Commission.

My gun crew was augmented to 40 men including a radioman. The Italians agreed to stay aboard for one more voyage. United States Navy officers came aboard as advisors to the Captain of the vessel. Approximately 2,000 men from the Army Air Corps came aboard as passengers and the Saturnia was bound for England. The Saturnia was propelled by electric diesel engines and traveled at more than 38 knots speed.

We arrived a week later at the King George's Docks at London, England and disembarked our passengers.

We were there for 4 days and witnessed the V-2 rocket bombs that were the nemesis of the English people.

We had two 3-inch 50s and 4 20-mm anti–aircraft weapons aboard. We assisted the London Port in defending the port. Half of my men joined the ATS Woman's Auxiliaries in raising and lowering the barrage balloons.

We returned directly to New York and the Saturnia was turned over to the U.S. Maritime Commission. My crew and I were returned to the Armed Guard Center in Brooklyn, for reassignment.

I was then assigned to a new Liberty ship, the Hannibal Hamlin (named for Abraham Lincoln's first-term Vice President). I had a crew of 16 men and for the first time a US Navy Line Officer Ensign assigned to command our

Chapter Four Into the Navy

crew. His name was Fischer Ames Buell from Oil Lyme, Connecticut.

The ship had a 5-inch 38 on the stern gun deck, a 3-inch 50 at the bow and 4 10-20-mm; two were located on each side of the ridge and two just forward of the stern gun deck. Our ship was fully loaded with cargo being sent to Russia.

We left our American port and proceeded to Halifax, Nova Scotia to join a convoy of more than 400 vessels to cross the north Atlantic. Some were headed for Scotland and the rest to Russia via the Artic Circle. We must have lost half the ships in the crossing being sunk by German submarine wolf packs and German dive bombers out of Norway.

The convoy to Russia went far north before turning to go south to Murmansk. The weather was so cold that the lubricants on our guns became frozen and I had to use blow torches to loosen up the lubricant. As we neared Russia, we were hit by two bombs in the forward section of our vessel by Stuka dive bombers. Although shrapnel fell like rain on Hannibal Hamlin the ship made it into the Russian port in one piece.

As the cargo was discharged, Russian women welders came aboard and welded new steel plates over the damaged portions of our bomb damaged decks. We returned to the United States and I requested a transfer into the larger Navy ships. I was promoted to Gunner's Mate 1-C in early 1943.

I was blessed in that I had survived so many times from enemy action and believed I had an angel on my shoulder. I was sent to the United States Naval Gun Factory at

USS *Duluth*, CL 87

Chapter Four Into the Navy

Anacostia for training on some of our new type weapons. Anacostia is on the east side of the District of Colombia.

I was there for 4 months while my new ship, the USS Duluth, CL-87, was being built at Newport News, Virginia. The Duluth was commissioned at Newport News Virginia in April 1943.

It started on its shakedown cruise in May and arrived at the Naval Torpedo Station in Newport, Rhode Island and tied up at the north mooring buoy on 5 June 1943.

Chapter Five
Out to Sea and Errol Flynn

Chapter Five Out to Sea and Errol Flynn

My home port was Newport, Rhode Island where my parents resided. I made a telephone call from the ship to my home. My father answered the phone and asked me where I was. I told him my ship had just tied up to the buoy just north of the torpedo station. He asked how long we would be there and if I could get liberty that night. I told him yes and he said he would meet me at the pier and that we would be going to the Lodge. I asked him, "What is the Lodge?" and he said, "You will soon know." He picked me up in his car and we went into Central Newport to a Masonic meeting at St. Paul's Lodge #14. There were 6 other members of our ship's crew at that meeting. Since we were only going to be in port for 10 days and my father had submitted my application to join the Masons as did my fellow crew members, we received our First Entered Apprentice Degree at St. Paul's Lodge, Newport. Three days later we attended the St. Paul #5 Masonic Lodge and with the help of guides assisting us, we received our second Masonic Fellow Kraft Degree. Four days later we returned to my father's lodge, St. Paul #14, and received our third Masonic Degree as a Master Mason on 14 June 1943.

We left Newport two days later and proceeded south through the Panama Canal and headed to the South China Sea in time to participate in the battle to liberate the Philippines. We were part of Admiral Spruance's 7th Fleet.

During the next year we participated in recovering much of the far eastern territories from the Japanese, i.e., Truk Lagoon, Tarawa, Guam, Iwo Jima, and Okinawa. After Okinawa, the 3rd Fleet under Vice Admiral William F. "Bull" Halsey, Jr., was proceeding north to attack the home islands of Japan. On 5 June, a major typhoon overtook the 3rd Fleet which was traveling at 20 knots.

The 3rd Fleet included more than 400 naval ships including support vessels.

The ships had to maintain their speed and course so that they would not hit each other. This contributed to the damages of the naval vessels. Aircraft carriers had their forward flight deck peeled back like a slipper and many damaged aircrafts. The USS Pittsburgh, a heavy cruiser, received major damage approximately 50 feet of the Pittsburgh bow was torn and sheared from the rest of the vessel. His bow section of the USS Pittsburgh remained afloat since all water tight hatches in the bow were sealed tight and the bow remained afloat. The USS Duluth had also received major damage to its bow. With sides of the holes to both port and starboard, opened up by the heavy seas, were big enough for a sailor to step

Chapter Five Out to Sea and Errol Flynn

through the hull to the outside. We were asked by Fleet Commander to take the USS Pittsburgh's bow in tow and return it to Guam for repair. When the typhoon finally passed, the USS Duluth and several damaged ships made their way to Guam for repairs.

I was sent by the Commanding Officer of the USS Duluth in a whale boat transporting a portion of the 4-inch hawser that had been previously secured to the stern of the USS Duluth to attach it to the bow of the USS Pittsburgh. This amazing feat was accomplished and the USS Duluth successfully towed the bow to Guam where repairs were made in July, 1945.

While we waited for repairs to our vessels to be completed, an announcement came over the ship's PA system requesting that all Master Masons in the 3rd Fleet were to report to the main mess hall on Guam to attend a Masonic Square and Compass meeting.

Admiral Halsey, a 33rd Degree Mason chaired the meeting that day and instructed the Masons on the proper wearing of the Masonic ring.

Americans had recaptured the Island of Guam the previous August. A Japanese holdout sniper in the hills was still shooting at the men working on the ships.

Shortly after the Duluth arrived, a spotter located a holdout sniper near a bamboo Nepa hut. My gun crew and I were sent to capture or kill them. We surrounded the hut and found a woman on the floor crying 'I'm hurt, I'm hurt."

When I moved down to see where she was hurt, a trap door opened up and a Jap came out with a knife. I reached up quickly to grab the man's wrist but grabbed the knife and twisted it out of his grasp, and stuck him in the stomach. I'm sure he had threatened the woman into acting as a decoy.

During the war I shot at a lot of planes and ships, but that is the only enemy soldier I'm certain I killed face-to-face.

Once the repairs were complete the Duluth rejoined the 3rd fleet which had entered Tokyo Bay. Following the dropping of the Atomic bomb on Hiroshima, the Japanese High Command surrendered to General MacArthur aboard the USS Missouri.

Following he surrender of the Japanese at Tokyo Bay, I received orders from the United States Navy Department transferring me from the USS Duluth to the United States Navy Gun Factory at Anacostia Naval base, Washington, D.C. I was flown to Pearl Harbor from Okinawa, Japan 10 September 1945. I then traveled aboard the USS Wasp, an aircraft carrier, arriving at Oakland, California 15 September.

I spent two days at a motel at Jack London Square and obtained my railroad ticket from Oakland to New York City.

A Chief Bosons Mate from another ship was traveling the same route to New York. We decided to share a compartment for the trip east. Our trip was delayed due to the Mississippi flooding. We continued to Chicago where we changed trains, then traveled to Grand Central Station in New York.

I said goodbye to the Chief and traveled on to Providence, Rhode Island and to Newport arriving there on 1 November 1945. After two weeks of leave, I reported

Chapter Five Out to Sea and Errol Flynn

into the United States Navy Base, Anacostia, Washington, D.C. My assignment was to the pre-commissioning detail to the USS Fresno, CL-121, which was being built at Newport News, Virginia. This new cruiser would carry a new type main battery which would be rapid fire 8-inch guns. My specific assignment there would be to see how the 8-inch guns were made and operated. I was to remain at the Naval Gun Factory for 6 months. Therefore, I rented an apartment nearby.

I reported to the USS Fresno on 5 March 1946 and was present for its launching the next day at Kearney, New Jersey. The ship was commissioned at the Brooklyn Navy Yard, New York 26 November 1946. The Fresno went to Bayonne, New Jersey to receive the new 8-inch rapid fire cannons. The departure date from the states was 13 January 1947, with orders to proceed to Guantanamo Bay, Cuba where she would undergo a shakedown training period for 10 weeks. I was very excited about this new opportunity and was delighted to accept.

The Fresno proceeded on a two month shakedown cruise which included testing all engines, radar, and equipment aboard. We also tested all of our 5 inch guns, 8 inch guns, 20-mm and 40-mm weapons, etc. Upon satisfactorily completing all tests during our shakedown cruise, the Fresno received orders to proceed south on a goodwill cruise around South America.

One first stop was the U.S. Naval Base, Guantanamo Bay, Cuba, then to the Island of Jamaica. We dropped anchor outside of the Port of Kingston. I noticed a cousin, Abe Issa, who was a very prominent businessman on the Island of Jamaica. I told him that my ship, the new USS

Fresno, was anchored off shore from the Port of Kingston. He asked me to come to dinner that night at Montego Bay and he would send a car for me. When I arrived at the pier of Kingston, I was told that the beautiful sailing yacht out in the harbor was owned by Errol Flynn, the actor of many adventure films.

When I arrived at Abe's hotel I was taken to a big dining room where Abe met me. He said that he had arranged for a family friend to be my companion and should be seated to his left at the table. Her name was Pamela Coxe and she was the daughter of the manager of the Reynolds Aluminum Mines on Jamaica. She was a young 16-year-old strawberry blonde with freckles and a cute dimple. We became great friends. Abe then introduced me to a gentleman on his right who turned out to be Errol Flynn. Mr. Flynn asked if I was from the new light cruiser that was anchored off the stern of his ship. He also issued a verbal invitation to me to visit his yacht.

The next day, accompanied by the Executive and two other officers from the USS Fresno, we took our ship's motor launch and went to visit Mr. Flynn's vessel. Imagine my surprise when I found my friend Pamela Coxe was also on board as a guest. She and I would remain friends for over 50 years.

After leaving Jamaica, we made goodwill stops at Havana and Rio de Janeiro. While at Rio I visited the Statue of Christ which stands at the top of Corcovado Mountain with Arms outstretched, blessing all who come to Rio de Janeiro. When I went through the tunnel I inscribed my name and date on the wall at the right side as I was traveling up to the statue.

CHAPTER FIVE OUT TO SEA AND ERROL FLYNN

U.S.S. Fresno in Rio de Janero

We continued south and entered the estuary of the River Platte. On entering the estuary we passed the hull of the German battleship, the Admiral Graf Spee, which had been scuttled there by its Captain Langsdorff, in 1941. On orders of Captain Langsdorff who had determined that his ship was totally blocked by the British Navy vessels at the port entrance and had it scuttled, so the British Navy could not capture it. His entire crew officers and men were sent ashore and interned in Uruguay. Then Captain Langsdorff went ashore and knelt down over his battle flag, took out his pistol and took his life as a matter of honor to show he was not a coward. Please note there was breaking news today, 10 November 2014, a German group is planning to re-float the Admiral Graf Spee and return it to Germany.

Our next stop was Buenos Aires, Uruguay where we had four days of liberty in a very beautiful port. We then went south and rounded Cap Horn, and went north to Santiago, Chile, our next liberty port. We spent two days there. We went north stopping at Lima, Peru then up to San Diego, California.

The Fresno's skipper asked me to his cabin and asked me to ship over for another 4 years. I told him I had no desire to remain in the Navy but wanted to go back to my home and continue my college education. He offered me a commission if I would remain aboard, but I wasn't interested.

I was transferred in June 1947 by the United States Navy to the destroyer John W. Weeks, DD-701, stationed at Alexandria, Louisiana to close out my Navy career as a training instructor in the southeastern USA. I received

Chapter Five Out to Sea and Errol Flynn

my honorable discharge from the United States Navy at Pensacola, Florida 28 November 1947. I traveled back to Newport by train.

While on the train heading home from Pensacola, Florida the train stopped at Grand Central Station in New York.

For 30 minutes I took that opportunity to call my grandmother who had her business showroom and offices in New Haven, Connecticut. I told her I was on my way home to Newport, Rhode Island. She told me my family no longer lived in Newport and I should get off the train n New Haven where she would send a car to bring me to her offices. When I arrived there she informed me that my parents were living about 10 miles away in Branford, Connecticut.

After being reunited with my family in Branford I spent many hours reviewing my options on how on get with my life. I loved the new location where my parents lived which was about 100 yards from Long Island Sound at a place called Indian Neck. My grandmother had many contacts with Yale University in New Haven and urged me to consider entering Yale. She also offered me employment in her company so I could earn some income. In order to do that, and start my education, I decided to attend a New Haven college associated with Yale called Quinnipiac College.

Utilizing the World War II Veteran GI bill, the college registrar said that I would need a high school diploma to enter Quinnipiac. They encouraged me to take the Connecticut State examination to obtain a GED diploma. This I did and was accepted at Quinnipiac taking night

U.S.S. Fresno

CHAPTER FIVE OUT TO SEA AND ERROL FLYNN

courses so I could earn a living at the same time. In two years I completed all the courses for an A. A. with an emphasis on law. My law professor encouraged me to enter the law school at Yale and continue a law career. He offered to introduce me to the Dean of the Yale Law School. I became a member of the debating team at Yale. With the urging of two professors at Yale who had befriended me Dr. John Brubatcher, Dean of the School of Education, and Dr. Millar Burrorghs, Dean of the School of Theology.

I participated on the local radio station, W.E.L.I. had a program discussing world affairs. I was arguing the perils of the proposed establishment of a Jewish homeland in Palestine which was already occupied by the Palestinians. Both Professors Brubatcher and Burroughs had recently returned from Lebanon, where they had attended the American University of Beirut (A.U.B.) for their sabbatical leave. They assisted me with research in preparing for my talks on the radio. They further strongly suggested I should consider going to A.U.B. in Lebanon to get my Masters Degree and round out my education. At this time I had also been elected to be President of the Syrian and Lebanese Club of New Haven.

I received a telephone call from Dr. Burroughs inviting me and my parents to attend a luncheon at Yale University where the guest speaker would be Dr. Steven Penrose, President of A.U.B. He spoke with my parents and me after the luncheon. He said he would welcome me to A.U.B. and that he heard many positive comments about me from Professors Brubatcher and Burroughs.

I also met a female student, Lilly Asfour, at the luncheon

who was studying at Yale. She told me her family lived close to A.U.B. My parents invited Miss Asfour to dinner at our home in Indian Neck. Soon she became a member of my family.

When I asked my father who he could remember in Baskinta, he told me he could only remember his first cousin, Aziz.

I filled out an application to attend A.U.B. for my MA and gave it to Dr. Penrose. Two weeks later I received a cable from the Registrar, Farid Fuleihan, of A.U.B. He denied my application saying there were many universities in the United States available to me and if I allowed you to enter A.U.B. you would be taking the place of an Arab student at the University. Dr. Penrose stated he understood the position Farid had taken. Dr. Penrose suggested that I attend a University chartered by the State of New York for one semester and then requested transfer to A.U.B. to complete my degree. The reason for this action is because A.U.B. was chartered by the same Board of Regions in the State of New York.

I applied to Columbia and New York University and was accepted at both. I selected New York University, School of Law. I attended NYU in 1953 for two semesters. I then requested transfer to A.U.B. While I was at NYU my counselor gave me a special assignment to study the United Nations Security Council proceedings. I sat in the Security Council at the back seat of the Lebanese delegation, listening, and making notes of the discussions.

Chapter Five Out to Sea and Errol Flynn

Chapter Six
BASKINTA

CHAPTER SIX BASKINTA

One afternoon, during a recess, I went out into the delegates' lounge to review my notes. A gentleman came and sat down next to me and introduced himself. I was surprised to recognize the Ambassador from Russia, Andre Vischenski. He said that he had seen me seated with the Lebanese delegation, and while smiling, asked what I was writing in my pretty red book. I was a little embarrassed, closed my notebook, and said it was an honor to meet his Excellency.

The head of the Lebanese Delegation was Ambassador Charles Malik. He was a renowned philosopher, and had also been President of the United Nations Security Council. I had been very impressed by the inter-play between him and the Ambassador Abba-Ehan of Israel.

In 1954, I arrived in Beirut, Lebanon and appeared at the Registrar's office and presented my documentation and application to attend the School of Political Science with a major in International Law; I was excited to learn that Professor Charles Malik had also returned to A.U.B.

that year and taught the class on Philosophy. He was very impressive and his teachings still live with me today.

When I arrived in Lebanon at the end of August 1954, I was met at the Beirut Airport by the Asfour family. They helped me get an apartment on Rue J'n Darc, which was outside the main gate of A.U.B. I also met another cousin, Richard "Dick" Freije, who was born in Syracuse, New York. He took me to meet his sister, Leila, who was head librarian of A.U.B. I told Dick I had attended a farewell dinner at the home of my uncle Wilfred in Utica, New York with my father. I had brought a small tape recorder with me and many of the relatives there took the opportunity to send messages to their relatives in Baskinta, Lebanon. Many of them also gave me sealed envelopes containing money gifts addressed to their relatives to be delivered by me to them. Some of the classic beautiful women of the world are found in Lebanon known as Canaan in the Bible as atested to by Omar Sheriff (Shaloub) George Clooney, and Maurice Hyder, age 93 and still looking.

Baskinta is a very lovely remote mountain village at 5,000 feet elevation in the Jeba-Sunnine Mountains rising more than 12,000 feet, east of Beirut with a population of over 6,000. The peaks of Mt. Sunnine are covered with snow year round. The French trained their ski troops during World War II on Mt. Sunnine.

In researching history of the Middle East, it was noted that King Nebuchadnezzar of Baghdad would annually send a caravan from Baghdad to Beirut, Lebanon to bring back to Baghdad many kegs and cachets of their famous wines for which (Lebanon and Canaan) were noted. Today wines are still exported from Lebanon throughout the Mediterranean. One of the famous vintners there who exported wine is the Ksara Winery. They also produce Lebanon's famous beverage, Arak.

About 2,000 feet above Baskinta, there was a spring called Nabah-Sunnine. The temperature of this spring was constantly at or below 32 degrees. It was said if you stropped a watermelon into the spring, it would split open from the extreme cold. It was said that the water from the spring which originated from the snow on the mountain traveled underground from that spring for more than 25 miles becoming a river called the Dog River for approximately one mile. (Nahar-Al-Kalb) emptying into the Mediterranean at the Bay of Jounieh. Above the Bay of Jounieh at the eastern end of the Mediterranean Sea is a large opening called the Cane of the Dog River (Nahar-Al-Kalb) emptying into the Mediterranean at the Bay of Jounieh at the eastern end of the Mediterranean Sea. The Dog River is Nava coble up in the mountain for small boats and canoes for approximately one mile. The opening of the cave is about 25 feet wide at the entrance; there are both stalagmites and stalactites inside the cave area.

There are plaques mounted in the walls of the cave as entrance as far as a man could go by small motorized boat and canoes. Among these is Alexander the Great, several Cesars from Italy and Rome, and many other world explorers. Today it is a major tourist attraction and is illuminated underground with colorful lights.

About a month after my arrival in Lebanon I asked Dick if he would take me to Baskinta to meet my father's relatives. We left Beirut on a Saturday morning about 9:00 a.m. proceeding north along the Mediterranean coast to a village called Antelias, and then turned east up the mountain. We passed through Bikfaya, Konchara at Btegrine, the road which was down to 1-1/2 lanes wide, then crossed the bottom of a deep gorge called Wadi El Jamejime (Valley of Skulls).

We then zigzagged north up the mountain to the top of the ride to the village of Kfarab, the ancestral home of the Maloufs. We turned east and continued up the ridge to Baskinta.

It was said the Christians used to pile stones near the village at the top of the ridge. When there was an attempt to attack the village, they would roll stones down on the enemies; hence the valley received the name The Valley of the Skulls.

In the American Embassy brochure on Lebanon, it did list the Baskinta area as one of the most beautiful areas where the cedars of Lebanon still exist. There were terraces of fruit trees on the mountain side which produced cherries, plums, peaches, and apples of all varieties. This fruit was major export items from Lebanon to the Arabian Peninsula.

We arrived at the main cafe' in the center of Baskinta. We stopped next to an open cafe'. Dick stood up and addressed the occupants of the cafe' All the cafe' tables were occupied by men drinking coffee and smoking. Dick's car was a convertible and we stopped next to the curb and the nearest tables were only three feet away. All of the occupants of the cafe' were looking at us expressing curiosity as to why we were there. Dick stood up and told the occupants we were there looking for Aziz Abouhaider. They seemed to ignore us. Dick repeated the request and asked for directions to Azia's home. Again they ignored us. I told Dick under the circumstances

Chapter Six Baskinta

we should return to Beirut.

At that moment I noticed a gentleman coming down the hill approaching the car. Our eyes met and I recognized Edmund who was the head teacher at the school in Baskinta. We had met at Binghamton, New York where he had been visiting relatives. He came to the car and hugged me and asked what was going on. I explained to him that I was a student at A.U.B. and had come to Baskinta to meet my relatives here and my father had asked me to locate his cousin, Aziz.

Edmund faced the people in the cafe' and was very agitated. He spoke loudly and said, "What the matter with you people? Your cousin from America has come to meet his relatives in Baskinta." He then turned to a man at the closest table pointing at him, and said, "Aziz, he asked for you and you ignored him?" Then he and many others started to cry in their embarrassment.

Dick asked Ariz if he would join us in the car so we could go up to his house. His brothers, Chafik and Tewfik, also joined us and said we should go to his home first, which we did. Dick explained to them that I had messages and envelopes for a number of family members and would like to deliver them.

By this time the entire village had heard about our arrival and gathered outside Chafik's home. Dick became the Master of Ceremonies delivering the message and envelopes to the appropriate people.

Most of the people left after the envelopes and messages were given. Then Aziz and Chafik expressed anger at my father for not informing them in advance of my pending arrival so that they could prepare a proper welcome.

Then I told them Dick and I had to get back to

Beirut for classes at A.U.B. and had to prepare for them. They wanted me to return next weekend so they could receive me properly. I turned to Dick and asked if he could bring me again and he agreed. We then returned to Beirut.

The next Saturday morning we headed for Baskinta. Again we turned right at Antelias. When we reached the village Bikfaya church bells began to ring. The same thing happened when we reached Konchara and Btegarine.

Dick said, "Maurice that's not a coincidence; they are ringing the bells to welcome you."

As we arrived at the top of the ridge beyond Kfarab heading toward Baskinta, all the village church bells were ringing.

All the village church bells were ringing. We drove around the next curve and were confronted with more than 1,000 people who filled the roadway. The priest from my father's church where he was baptized stepped forward and held a prayer service welcoming Dick and me to Baskinta. I was picked up and carried on the shoulders of my cousins and carried to Chafik's home where a feast had been prepared.

In the evening Dick and I sat with my male cousins eating mezza and drinking Arak, toasting each other. The women folk were in the kitchen or standing in a room behind the men providing food.

After three hours of drinking Arak, the wife of Aziz, said, "You should be ashamed of yourselves trying to get your cousin drunk," since by this time some of the men had passed out. Chafik asked me if I had drunk much Arak before.

I told him that my uncles had made their own Arak back in the United States and that I assisted them, and

Chapter Six Baskinta

had some at every dinner. Dick and I returned to Beirut on Sunday.

On 1 September 1955 I made another trip to Baskinta in a taxi that provided daily round trips. The driver of the taxi was my cousin, Shaeen. I asked him on the trip did they have many accidents on this narrow dangerous road.

He said, "All the good drivers make it; the bad drivers don't.!"

Chapter Seven
The New F.S.O.

Chapter Seven The New F.S.O.

When I was living with my family in Branford, Connecticut I had joined a theater company as a volunteer at Stanford. I was an understudy to the make-up person and assisted him with the cast of the production. With the help of the make-up professional, I obtained a complete make-up kit with the necessary contents thereof. I took my make-up kit with me to Beirut where I joined the American Community Theatrical Guild and received $25.00 per production when I provided make-up for them.

In November 1955 while providing make-up for Roger Abraham, the Administrative Officer of the American Embassy at Beirut, I asked him if there were any jobs I could perform at the American Embassy. He asked me what my problem was.

I told him that I was going to A.U.B. under the GI bill which paid all my tuition costs but only provided $75.00 per month to live on. I told him I couldn't get from my apartment to the university without passing someone I owed money to and needed to find a way to earn more income. He said, "Come to the Embassy tomorrow and we will discuss it."

I went to the Embassy the next day and met with Roger. He told me that they had a vacancy and if I was interested, he could put me in that position. I asked him if it paid money, I will take it.

He laughed and said, "Yes, but you should know that the last two occupants of that position had quit the Embassy and returned to America and said "I would do my best for the Embassy."

My new title would be Property Officer and End-Use Auditor. My job would be to go out into the Lebanon countryside, locate equipment that was provided to Lebanon under the Marshall Plan, and if possible, provide photos thereof.

After two days of research of the Embassy documents pertaining to such equipment I proceeded to a village in the Bekaa Valley. When I arrived there I approached the village leader. He asked me what I wanted looking me over very carefully. I told him that his village had received equipment provided by the United States and I wanted to see them and take photos. He said others had come and he had sent them away.

Then he said, "You look like a son of Lebanon" and he asked "What was your name again?"

I told him I was Maurice Hyder of the American Embassy in Beirut.

He then asked me what was my father's name and what village did he come from.

Chapter Seven The New F.S.O.

I told him Charles Hyder who had immigrated to the United States from the Village of Baskinta.

He said, "You are not Hyder; you are Abou-Haider and you are a cousin." He said, "Come, I'll show you everything and take whatever pictures you want to." I returned to the American Embassy and showed the Administration Officer my report and the pictures I had taken. He was excited at my progress and said the Ambassador would like to see what I had accomplished and took me to his office.

The Ambassador said, "You've got everything I need to respond to the American Congress."

He congratulated me and said, "We need you in the State Department; are you interested?"

At this time I was a Contract Employee of the American Embassy and said I would be interested if it could be arranged. The Administrative Officer gave me an application to become a Foreign Service Officer of the United States Department of State. The Ambassador submitted my application to the United States Department in Washington, D.C. with his endorsement.

A few days later the Ambassador called me to his office and said he had received a response from the State Department, which advised him that I was qualified but could not be accepted as an Intern because I was over the age of 31 which was the maximum age for new Interns. The Ambassador told me not to worry; the State Department owed him many favors as he would make arrangements for me.

A few weeks later I received a letter from the United States Department of State which stated upon satisfactory completion of my education at A.U.B., I should report to the United States Department in November, 1956, to attend the Foreign Service Institute (F.S.I.). I continued to work at the American Embassy as a Contract Officer through 1955 and up to 30 June 1956 when I would return back to the United States.

In June 1956, I had been told that I had completed my work for my Masters Degree. Imagine my surprise when I checked the bulletin board announcing those who would be receiving their degrees at the graduation ceremonies on 1 July, and my name was not there! I went to the Registrar and asked Mr. Farid Fuleihan why my name was not on the graduation list since I had completed all my requirements satisfactorily. He told me that he had registered me as a special student and I was not in a degree program. Needless to say, I was very upset.

On 25 June 1956, I went to see Dr. Edw. McDonald, the Education Advisor of USAID at the American Embassy in Beirut. I told him everything that had transpired from the time I applied to A.U.B. and the completion of my educational requirements for my Masters Degree. He listened very carefully and advised me to go back to my apartment nearby and that I would be contacted by the A.U.B. About 1300 hours that same day I was called by Prof. Kosti Zuryak, the Acting President of A.U.B. asking if I would allow representatives of A.U.B.'s Executive Board to call upon me. I said yes.

Three members of the A.U.B. Executive Board came to my apartment and I invited them into my living room.

The spokesperson of the group told me that acting President Zuryak had sent them to apologize to me and

Chapter Seven The New F.S.O.

that an error by A.U.B. had led to the misunderstanding. Further I would receive my Masters Degree on 1 July and would be presented to me by the President to me personally at the graduation ceremony.

They asked me to withdraw my complaint against A.U.B.

I called Ed McDonald and thanked him for his intercession with the A.U.B. and my case and asked what had happened.

He told me he had called concerning the accreditation of the A.U.B. Charter which could be revoked since A.U.B. received its charter under the State of New York, Board of Regions. Since A.U.B. had been accepting payments from the United States government under Public Law 480 for my education which could only be legal under the United States Congress G.I. Bill Law, used for a degree program.

I found myself accepted by most of the students of the University. They engaged me in many discussions in the cafeteria and on the campus. It helped me to get a quicker and comprehensive understanding of their family life and concerns.

I also had an opportunity to meet many of their families who asked questions about places in America where some of their families resided. It was of interest to me to note that a large percentage of the students all had cell phones. Their parents told me that was how they kept track of their children, by the cell phone.

On 1 July the A.U.B. had their graduation ceremony. All diplomas were presented to the appropriate persons by the A.U.B. officials while I waited patiently. I was finally called to the podium and received my diploma by the

Acting President, Kosti Zuryak.

The Political Science club met later that afternoon at San Simone Beach south of Beirut. We had planned an American style hot dog and hamburger party with our parents and guests attending. I was told by friends of mine they had arranged a blind date for me; her name was Sheila Howard. I was working on the barbeque.

Two of my classmates came to me and said they would take over the barbeque because Sheila was coming through the beach tunnel from the highway. I hadn't met her previously so I went 20 feet up into the tunnel and when a young lady that looked "American" approached, I said, "Hi Sheila, I'm Maurice;" the young lady pushed her hand up with her thumb pointing behind her saying, "I'm not Sheila; she's behind me." I was a little embarrassed and greeted the American young lady and greeted her in the same manner. She told me she knew who I was and with her nose in the air, she walked right past me. I went back to my job at the barbeque pit.

I spent 2nd and 3rd of July packing my bags for the upcoming trip to Jerusalem and Egypt to visit my grandmother's relatives. On 4 July at 1:00 p.m. the American Embassy residence became the site of our Independence Day celebration. All senior members of the diplomatic and commercial establishments came to the Ambassador's residence to pay their respects to him on our national day.

The Embassy grounds were festively decorated and hors d'oeuvres and beverages were shared with all attendees. As a member of the Embassy staff, I was required to meet newcomers and make them welcome.

Chapter Seven The New F.S.O.

Chapter Eight
Sheila

Chapter Eight Sheila

About 3:30 p.m. someone came up behind me, tapped me on the shoulder, and I was surprised to see Sheila standing next to me.

I greeted her and said, "Welcome. What can I do for you?"

She said, "Nothing but I want to apologize to you."

I asked, "For what?"

"When I met you at your A.U.B. party, I acted impulsively because so many of my friends had told me that you were much too old for me and had a bad reputation. They reminded me about the notice that had been placed on the Beirut Women's College (B.C.W.) bulletin board that your apartment was out of bounds for all students at B.C.W."

She told me that her parents had taught her better manners and asked if we could start over again and invited me to meet her friends at the restaurant in front of the main gate at A.U.B.

After I left the U.S. Embassy party, I told her I would try to be there about 5:00 p.m. I arrived there about 5:15 and was introduced to all. The female friends of Sheila's greeted me warmly. The male attendees greeted me with suspicion and hostility.

Sheila asked me if I could join her friend at her parents' chalet at San Simon Beach for the next day at 1900 p.m.; Sheila and I had many opportunities to discuss our backgrounds, future hopes, and ultimate goals. She told me she would drop me off at my apartment in Beirut when everybody went home after the party. She also invited me to join her family for dinner that evening.

From that point on it seemed that we were together at various activities for the next seven days. She came to my apartment and helped me pack up my belongings in preparation for my return to the United States. I told her I had scheduled a trip to Jerusalem and Cairo, Egypt to visit my grandmother's relatives and would be returning to Beirut five days later. She said she would miss me and would meet me at the Beirut Airport when I returned.

At Cairo, Egypt I met my grandmother's niece and nephews: Selim, George, and Nadia Malouf. My cousins took me on a tour of Cairo and arranged for me to take a camel around the Great Sphinx and the Great Pyramids.

When I returned to Beirut, Sheila was waiting for me at the airport. I asked her to drop me off at a hotel. She said that wouldn't be necessary since her mother had insisted that I would be their houseguest for the next three days prior to my departure to my home in the United States. It was a wonderful visit and time to get acquainted with her parents.

Chapter Eight Sheila

I arrived at New York around 15 July and was met by my brothers, Fred and Richard, who took me to my home in Connecticut.

I was very excited to see my parents and grandmother spending many hours telling them about my experiences in Lebanon. It was fun sharing the highlights with my siblings and cousins of those experiences.

On 10 August I received a letter from the United States Department confirming my appointment to the State Department. I was instructed to report to the Foreign Service Institute in Washington, D.C. on 1 November 1956. They tested my knowledge of the Middle East. I was challenged by other Foreign Service Officers on political, sensitive issues and my position thereto. I was also given many documents to read on United States Foreign Service Policy with regard to situations in the Middle East.

On 20 November I was told that my first post would be to the Government in Libya. I was given copies of the Libyan Post Report, possible living conditions, and the status of the political situation in Libya.

I left Washington by Pan American Air. My first stop was London, England, then to B.E.A., arriving at Tripoli, Libya on 20 December 1956. I spent Christmas at Tripoli and on 15 January was assigned to Benghazi as the General Services Officer (G.S.O.) which provided most of the administrative services at that post. My responsibilities there would be the administrative support of the Benghazi Post. This would include housing for all of the Americans assigned there, motor pool, vehicles, travel coordinator, procurement, and contracting of the post. My supervisor was the Executive Officer here at Tripoli.

Upon arrival I purchased a Sunbeam Rapier sports car.

I found out that I was the only bachelor at the post. As a result, my living quarters were on the top floor of the Benghazi office building which comprised of one bedroom, bath, and small living room. I hired a house boy to maintain the apartment. His name was Ali who had been born in Sudan. The rest of the staff were families with children and were located within five miles of the office building, mostly to the east of Benghazi.

Since I was living at the top of the office building, I automatically became the Duty Officer of the Benghazi Post. I soon met local higher Palestinians and Lebanese employees who befriended me. One of the Palestinians that I met, Michele Tubbeh, became a close personal friend.

Benghazi is located next to the Mediterranean Sea and had a large harbor. Two weeks after my arrival I bought an Arab 16 foot Felluca sailboat. It carried a lateen triangular (a lateen is a triangular sail set on a long yard mounted at an angle on the mast, running in a fore-and-aft direction; it is still used as a working rig by coastal fishermen in the Mediterranean) sail on a long spar which was attached to a short 8 foot mast. I used a steering oar at the stern. To the west of the harbor was a beautiful beach used by the Americans at the Post.

My primary recreation was sailing my boat out of the Benghazi Harbor along the Mediterranean coast. The name of my boat was the "Malesh." In English it means "What does it matter?" Sheila and I exchanged many letters and I invited her to come to Benghazi for a visit. She wrote and said she was coming to Benghazi with

Chapter Eight Sheila

her sister Anne as chaperone and would arrive 15 March. I purchased new linens and a bedspread to spruce up my apartment.

Before I went down to my office the next day I handed the linens and bedspread to Ali and told him to put the bedspread on the bed. Since my guests were arriving the next day I wanted to make a good impression. It was my practice to go up to my apartment for a beverage and a sandwich at lunch time.

On looking over everything I saw the bed without the bedspread and asked Ali "What did you do with the bedspread?" I told you to put it on the bed" He looked up at me and said, "I do as you say, Saah, I put it on the bed." I said, "I don't see it." He lifted up the mattress and there it was. I laughed at him and demonstrated how it should be done.

With the impending arrival of Sheila and Anne I was planning a welcoming party the next night and sent invitations to the Embassy staff and their wives to meet Sheila. Michele Tubbeh told me his wife and friends would cater the party. They did a great job providing Lebanese food and desserts. Mrs. Tubbeh also helped entertain the guests playing her Oud (mandolin)).

Michele also brought a durbakee (drum) and accompanied his wife on his instrument. There was much dancing and singing of Arabic songs. Sheila participated in the Dubkee line dance. Everyone had a great time.

The next day Ali told me that his friends who were servants in other American homes said the rumors were that Mr. Hyder had looked over is guests and was going to marry both of them.

I explained to Ali that I had made no such decision and that they were just friends of mine.

I took Sheila and Anne touring Cyrenaica up to the Egyptian border. They were very impressed with the ruins of the temples and statuary at Cyrene.

In the Bible we are told that a man from Cyrene named Simon helped Jesus when he stumbled as he carried the heavy cross on his way to the crucifixion. Simone took the weight of the cross on his shoulders and helped support Jesus on his way to Golgotha.

I enjoyed Sheila's visit very much; we had an opportunity to discuss our future. Before her departure, Sheila asked me to come to Beirut to visit her during the coming Easter holiday. I made plans to fly to Beirut for Easter. I also thanked Michele and his wife for their generous help during Sheila's visit.

Michele Tubbeh was the Administrative Assistant to the Crown Prince Sayed Abdullah of Libya. At the request of the Crown Prince he was asked to bring Mr. Hyder to the Palace so he could meet me. He asked me many questions about my life and the United States and we soon became very good friends.

He also introduced me to his father, King Idreiss, who invited me to stay for dinner at the Palace.

I flew to Beirut the Monday before Easter and was met by Sheila at the airport. During the next few days we discussed our developing relationship which was becoming more serious. I had called my cousin, Chafik at Baskinta, and he asked me to be there on Saturday to be the Godfather to his new son. I said I would be honored.

Sheila, who had her own car, drove me to Baskinta.

Chapter Eight Sheila

During the baptismal ceremony at the Orthodox Church while I was holding the baby, I experienced dizziness and asked my friend Philip who was standing next to me, to assist me as I was afraid I was going to lose control. He helped steady me by holding my arm under the baby. At the end of the baptismal service, the priest asked both Philip and I to sign the baptismal certificate since we were both holding the baby at the time of the baptism.

Sheila recognized I was having some difficulty and said we must return immediately to Beirut to see their family doctor.

The doctor was able to make an immediate diagnosis and said I was jaundiced and should be hospitalized. The Beirut Embassy put me on a plane directly to Tripoli, Libya where I entered the Air Force Hospital.

During the time I was with Sheila at her home in Beirut prior to the trip to Baskinta I had proposed marriage to her and she had said yes subject to her parents' approval. While I was at the hospital I received a letter from Sheila advising me that she would be accompanying her parents to New York where her father had official business with Chase Manhattan Bank. I sent a letter to her suggesting that if possible, she might take the opportunity to visit my parents in Branford, Connecticut, and that I would send a letter to my mother telling her about our marriage plans.

I recovered from hepatitis and returned to my post at Benghazi. While I was in the hospital I wrote a letter to my mother telling her my special friend Sheila who was visiting her, was going to become my wife, and then we were thinking we might take advantage of the coming Christmas holidays to get married.

My letter to my mother was delayed in getting to Connecticut.

Sheila had called my mother when she was in New York and told my mother that she met me in Beirut and we had become great friends. My mother was excited that someone who had known me in Beirut was calling to say hello and she immediately invited Sheila to visit our home in Branford, Connecticut to tell her about me. Sheila had assumed that my letter to my mother advising her about our wedding plans had already arrived.

Sheila arrived at the New Haven, Connecticut railroad station. My brother Fred met her and took her to our home at Indian Neck. He liked Sheila and made a play for her which Sheila rebuffed.

After four days of this inner-play, Fred asked Sheila if she was already committed to a boyfriend and Sheila said yes without further explanation. Fred said to her, "It couldn't be my brother, could it? Sheila smiled and said maybe.

My letter arrived on Friday. Fred steamed it open and read it, then resealed it and put it on the credenza. My grandmother noticed it on Saturday and recognized my writing style and knew it was from me, but did not open it because she couldn't read cursive, and stuffed it in the right side of her chair. Sheila's parents had planned to pick Sheila up from our home on the early afternoon of Sunday. Sheila was very upset that no one appeared to have received ay word from me regarding our future plans. With her parents' arrival, she didn't know what to do since it was expected that our parents would discuss our wedding plans.

Chapter Eight Sheila

Early Sunday morning my mother and grandmother did their usual things, baking bread and various Lebanese dishes. During a pause in their baking my grandmother told my mother that a letter had been received from Maurice.

My mother asked, "Where is it?" My grandmother said it was in the right side of her reclining chair.

My mother went and retrieved the letter and was shocked when she opened it and read the first sentence which said, "Mom, my friend, Sheila, who is visiting you, is going to be your new daughter-in-law. I have proposed marriage to her; she has said yes and her parents have approved."

My mother screamed and called out to my father who thought something bad had happened.

They sat together and read the entire letter.

My mother said, "We have to act quickly as Sheila's parents will be arriving this afternoon. We must have a family gathering to announce the engagement."

They immediately started calling the relatives asking them to be at the house by 1:00 p.m. to be there before Mr. and Mrs. Howard arrived.

Sheila got up, packed her bag, and started down the stairs at 9:15. When she reached the middle landing of the stairway, she saw my mother standing in the lower hallway at the bottom of the stairs with her hands on her hips looking up at Sheila, and said, "Young lady, what's this I hear?"

Sheila replied, "I don't know what you're talking about."

My mother replied, "You have been here for a week and I have just learned that you are going to marry my son,

Maurice." When Sheila got to the bottom of the steps my mother reached out and gave her a big hug.

She said, "I'm so happy for you and Maurice."

After breakfast Sheila was saying to herself, "I've got to get word to my parents before they meet the Hyders."

She had called them in New York and told them the letter from Maurice announcing our marriage plans had not yet been received. Dad and Mom Hyder went upstairs and got themselves ready to receive guests, who started to arrive at 11:30 a.m.

Sheila enjoyed meeting everyone but made sure she was near the home entrance facing the road so that she could intercept her parents when they arrived. Mr. and Mrs. Howard arrived at 2:00 p.m.

Sheila rushed out to give her mother a hug, and whispered in her ear, "They know, they know!"

My mother and father went down the front steps to meet the Howards and soon became great friends. My parents brought them into the house and introduced them to our family and relatives. This was followed by typical Lebanese customs which included toasting each family with Scotch and Arak, and a beautiful table of Lebanese mezza. They departed for New York about 6 p.m.

After an exchange of letters with Sheila, the wedding plans were underway. We had some difficulties determining what church in which we would be married. Since I was baptized Orthodox and Sheila was baptized Roman Catholic, she and I visited with the Irish priest of the Catholic Church they attended in Beirut and had not yet resolved our difficulties. He suggested that I seek counseling in Benghazi at the Cathedral with the Bishop

Chapter Eight Sheila

to resolve our religious differences.

Essentially his recommendation was based upon three issues:

(1) How often did I go to church versus how often did Sheila go to church;

(2) Did we plan to have children;

(3) Who would be taking the children to church? He told me I had answered my own questions. Sheila would have most of the religious responsibilities of the family and her wishes should come first. Accordingly, I notified Sheila I had withdrawn my religious position and would marry her in the Roman Catholic Church.

The date for our marriage was set. We were to be married on 27 December 1957. The marriage would take place at the Roman Catholic Cathedral in downtown Beirut, and the reception would be held at the Howard family penthouse in Ras, Beirut.

I made my arrangements to fly to Beirut on 24 December. Two United States Marines serviced our Embassy in Benghazi and agreed to drive my personal car to Cairo, Egypt.

The Theatre and the Intern In this manner it would be there when Sheila and I arrived in Cairo at the beginning of our honeymoon. The Marines had delivered my car in Abbas; the American Embassy had been closed due to the political situation in Egypt.

I stopped at Cairo during my flight from Benghazi to Beirut. Abbas came aboard the plane during my 15 minute layover at Cairo and handed me an envelope explaining that inside were prescriptions needed at the American Embassy at Cairo.

He said he'd meet me when I returned from Beirut with Sheila.

I was met at the Beirut International Airport by Sheila and her father's driver, Ameen, on 24 December and taken to the Howard residence. I gave the driver the envelope that Abbas had given me at Cairo and asked for his assistance in following the medical request.

The wedding went off on schedule. Mr. Howard's bank limousine took Sheila and me from the church to the Howard residence. Ameen also tied a series of empty cans to the rear bumper as he was told it was an American tradition.

Sheila's sister Anne was the maid of honor and joined us in the reception line at the Howard penthouse. My memory is that Sheila and I were in that reception line for three hours – from our arrival to our departure for our honeymoon.

Chapter Eight Sheila

Chapter Nine
Our Wedding

CHAPTER NINE OUR WEDDING

Our first night was at a hotel in Beirut. The next two days was back at the penthouse opening gifts and acknowledging them. One of our special gifts was a beautiful miniature poodle that we named "Coca," who would accompany us on our honeymoon. We left Beirut on 2 January for Cairo with our chaperone "Coca."

When our airplane arrived at Cairo International Airport it was met by the American Embassy limousine and was driven by Abbas. We were not at the receiving area at the airport but at a special diplomatic area. Abbas asked me if I had the requested package. I said, "Yes;" he said "to get into the car and come with him to the diplomatic reception area." On arrival I was introduced to the Foreign Minister of Egypt and the Chief of Egyptian Immigration. I was then told that the medication I had brought with me from Beirut was very critical for the medical treatment of their children and was no longer available in Egypt. They were very appreciative and said "every effort would be made to make our trip in Egypt very special."

Abbas confirmed that my car had arrived safely and was

parked at the American Embassy and would be available when I needed it. He then took us in the Samirmes Hotel on the Nile River. This hotel has appeared in many American movies and was a major tourist attraction.

When we arrived at the desk of the Concierge with Coca, he told us we could not bring a dog into his hotel. Abbas said "one moment, sir, may I use your phone?"

He spoke for about a minute and handed the phone to the concierge who looked at us in awe! "I'm sorry, Mr. Hyder, for having offended you. The owner of the hotel was on his way down to the lobby to meet Coca."

After a few minutes of conversation with Abbas, he told us he was very fond of poodles, that he would like to keep Coca in his penthouse until our return from our honeymoon, and that our suite at the hotel would be complimentary for us. Abbas said he made all necessary arrangements for our honeymoon and that the government of Egypt would host our trip to Egypt.

The next morning Abbas picked us up at the front door of the hotel with our suitcases.

We started south from Cairo and Sheila asked Abbas, "Where are we going?"

He said, "To see the wonders of Egypt;" and that all the details have been arranged.

He pulled up to a railroad crossing and stopped the car and offered us flutes of champagne and toasted our marriage. About five minutes later the train from Cairo came down the track, with a special Pullman car and stopped at the roailroad crossing.

Abbas said, "Your train is waiting for you."

He wished us well and said he would meet us on the return trip a week later.

CHAPTER NINE OUR WEDDING

Our Wedding Day

We continued our visit through Egypt up the Nile stopping at Luxor, the Valley of the Kings, and the Aswan Dam; we were wined and dined as guests of Egypt. At each stop we spent a few days and were escorted by guides from the Ministry of Tourism who provided us with a verbal history of Egypt. Many times we rode mules to reach points of interest.

We returned to Cairo six days later, and yes, the train stopped at our special railroad crossing. Abbas and the Embassy limousine were there to take us to our hotel. The next day we had a tour on camels to visit the Great Sphinx and the Pyramids.

While in Cairo we met my grandmother's niece and nephews, Nadia, Selim, and George Malouf. They took us shopping at the Souks of Old Time Cairo and purchased gifts for our families back home. We picked up our car, collected Coca, our chaperone, and gave the owner of the Samerimes Hotel a token gift and expressed our appreciation for his hospitality.

We headed west towards Benghazi. While enroute we were accosted by a violent sand storm which forced us off the road for safety. Our vision was reduced to a couple of feet and our small sports car was bounced back and forth b the wind. The storm passed within three hours. I went out to examine the car which was sitting in hit deep sand. The left side of the car had been sandblasted down to bare metal and we could not move without help.

An hour later an Egyptian truck arrived that pushed the sand off the road. They dug my car out and helped us get back on the road. We stopped at El Alamein where British General Montgomery had stopped General Rommel's advance towards Egypt, which was a major turning point

Chapter Nine Our Wedding

The Reception

Our Chariot Awaits

of the Nazi invasion of North Africa. We spent the night in Tobruk which had been the location of the German Mediterranean submarine fleet.

The longer I lived with Sheila I learned many things about her background. She was descended from the Bunker family that is mentioned in the history books. In the hardback Bunker Genealogy book that I now have in my possession in which Sheila and her sister, Anne, are listed in the last paragraph. They are descendants of the Huganauts of Northern France and William the Conqueror who conquered England.

They are also descendants of a Major of George Washington's Army of the American Revolution.

I'm sure that's why she was the gutsy girl that she illustrated during our life together.

The cuisine of Lebanon which originated thousands of years ago, as rated by the United Nations, is considered one of the most popular and healthiest food in the world; i.e. Tabouli, salad (parsley salad) containing cracked #1 fine bulgur (parsley, garlic, lemon juice, olive oil and spices, hummus, garbanzo beans, tahini sauce; babaghanooj, eggplant, garlic, olive oil, lemon juice, tahini and spices, etc. Recipes on the famous Lebanese foods can be found in every library.

The next day we stopped at Cyrene which had been a major city in the Roman Empire and now was in ruins. The heads of the statutes had been knocked off during the Moslem advance across North Africa. We arrived in Benghazi a few hours later and was met at our new home by all our friends from the Embassy, notably Peggy and Bill Doyle.

Chapter Nine Our Wedding

Chapter Ten
Our First Born
and the
Crown Prince

Chapter Ten Our First Born and the Crown Prince

A month later Sheila told me that she was pregnant; that she would be expected to deliver sometime in October, 1957. I took her sailing and Coca was aboard. At one point when I was making a full turn and the boom was swinging about, it hit Coca and swept him off into the sea. I was frightened and told Sheila to come about and I dove overboard to help Coca.

When I reached Coca he immediately tried to climb on top of my head. Sheila was panicked since I hadn't taught her how to sail the boat. I yelled to her to let go of the rope tied to the boom and the boat would automatically come up into the wind while I swam with Coca back to the boat. Coca was glad to be back on board and went to Sheila for comfort.

I continued to each Sheila about sail boat handling and returned back to Benghazi Harbor. Our days in Benghazi were very pleasant. I took opportunities to show Sheila all the sights in the Province of Cyrenaica. During one such trip eat we stopped just off the trip for lunch. I made sure we all stayed within 10 feet of the road since we had been warned that all belligerents had planted land mines as they retreated from a military confrontation. Imagine my surprise when I turned over nearby large stones to form a fire ring and found two Beretta pistols. They were 32 cal-9-mm. I kept the best one on my person from that moment on at all times. I became an expert on the firing range using my left hand.

With the help of my houseboy Ali, I developed a vegetable garden which produced tomatoes, cucumbers, peppers, and radishes. I told Ali that I had ordered some manure to enrich the soil of our garden which would arrive in a couple of days.

He asked me, "What is manure?"

I explained to him in Arabic Khatta, (t'was (SHIT) and he said, "Okay." He understood.

One of the activities that all of the Embassy wives participated in was the card game Bridge which would include a luncheon. They would be attended by 20 or more Embassy wives. Ali was the houseboy. At one of these luncheons Ali came to the dining room door, got Sheila's attention and told her that the truck ordered by Mr. Hyder had arrived and needed instruction. He told her a little too loudly a truck was outside the garden gate and had the item for the garden but couldn't say the word. Still confused, he told Sheila it was the "SHIT!"

Sheila was very embarrassed and told him it should be off-loaded near the garden and returned to her partner at the Bridge table.

Chapter Ten Our First Born and the Crown Prince

A few weeks later I needed to fly to our headquarters at Tripoli, Libya and Sheila drove me to the Benghazi Airport where I was to travel in a small two-person aircraft. As we drove off I realized I still had the keys to the car in my pocket, and Sheila was on the ground. We circled above the parking area and I took off my tie attaching the keys to it while the pilot revved the engine to get Sheila's attention. I waved to her and dropped the tie. I noticed her going to pick it up. On my return to Benghazi, Sheila told me that she asked one of the Embassy mechanics to show her how to hotwire the car so that she would never be caught unprepared again. She was one versatile4 female and I was proud of her. Sheila told me that her mother Helen and Aunt Bernice were coming to Benghazi in September to be with her during the birth of our child. Both Helen and Bernice were bridge buffs and fit in very well with her friends.

We did not have an Embassy Medical facility at Benghazi. Sheila's due date approached; her doctor told me to keep him advised on her condition. She was overdue; I thought a ride in the boat might help the situation along. My fellow colleague, Ted Brown, our police advisor, was my guest aboard; we cruised around Benghazi Harbor. Suddenly Sheila gave me a funny look and whispered to me that she thought she was beginning labor pains. I told everybody to hang on as I turned quickly to head back to the pier.

Ted asked me, "What is wrong?" I told him Sheila was starting to have labor pains.

He said, "You better get us ashore quickly."

Although he had been trained to assist in pregnancies

when he was Police Chief in Eugene, Oregon, he had never had to do so and didn't want to start now. We tied up to the pier, got Sheila into my car and went to the doctor's office in Benghazi.

That day was the 24th of October and also Sheila's birthday. I wondered at the significance of whether Sheila and the baby's birth would be on the same date. The doctor told me to stay at his office as Sheila had many hours to go and wanted me nearby to render assistance. While's Sheila's labor pains increased, she didn't deliver until 2:00 a.m. the next morning, the 25th of October.

The doctor delivered a 6 pound, 2 ounce, blonde, blue-eyed baby boy. Mother and baby were doing well. I was able to take Sheila and the baby to our home in Benghazi the next day since her mother and Bernice would be there to help care for her and the baby.

The baby would be named Mark Jay Hyder.

A week later my friend, the Crown Prince Syaed Abdullah of Libya, invited Sheila to the palace and asked her to bring our new son, Mark, with her to meet his wives. His wives and concubines were very excited about the visit and presented Mark with beautiful Libyan clothing and other gifts. Sheila's mother and Bernice who had accompanied her to the palace enjoyed their visit very much. Sheila extended a reciprocal invitation to the Prince's wives to visit our home in Benghazi during the following week. Invitations were also sent to the wives of the Embassy staff to attend.

That day when I left the office to go home, I was confronted at military checkpoints two blocks from my home. I realized this was standard procedure when the

Chapter Ten Our First Born and the Crown Prince

Prince's wives were nearby. I had to wait over two hours before the checkpoints were eliminated and I was allowed to go home. Upon my arrival I found Mark dressed in Libyan clothing and received a blow-by-blow description from Sheila and her mother of the day's events.

Our home leave date was approaching and Sheila decided to fly to Beirut with her mother on 1 December and I was to follow soon thereafter and arrived in Beirut on 15 December. I found Sheila in bed at Beirut where she was feeding Mark from a bottle with a prepared formula. During the coming travel, her doctor had recommended that feeding Mark with a bottle would be more preferable due to the constant change of travel conditions for both mother and baby. Our travel back to the United States included traveling by ship from Naples, Italy to New York aboard the SS Independence.

Sheila spoke to her mother and said, "Mom, we're going to be arriving in New York on 28 December and it is snowing and we're not accustomed to that. Do you think Dad can call his boss to expedite us upon our arrival in New York?"

His boss was Nelson Rockefeller who was the CEO at Chase Manhattan Bank and the American Export Line which owned the SS Independence. It was my understanding that mom asked her husband, "Frank, do you think you can help the kids?"

We had an early Christmas in Beirut and departed from Beirut via Pan Am to Rome on 20 December. We then traveled by train to Naples where we boarded the SS Independence. My immediate supervisor at the Benghazi Embassy was Dick Carhin who was also traveling aboard the Independence with his wife, Mary. We arranged with them to be seated at the same table for our meals during our trip to New York. This made for an enjoyable relationship aboard the ship.

Mark made his first appearance on deck during the first abandon ship drill. It appeared to others that Sheila was just holding a spare life vest in her hand, until she squeezed him and Mark let out a yell of protest. Mark was almost two months old.

We were enjoying our trip aboard when on the 24th of December the ship's Chief Purser knocked on our door and asked, "Mr. and Mrs. Hyder?"

I said "yes" then he asked, "*Who are you?*" I replied, "Nobody."

He said, "Ah ha. Then why is the Captain turning the ship upside down to accommodate you? The Captain wants you and your wife to be seated at his table on his left tonight at dinner. He also has instructed me to assign a shipboard nurse to your cabin to care for your baby for the duration of the voyage. The Captain has also arranged a special reception and dinner to introduce Mr. and Mrs. Hyder tomorrow at dinner."

The rumors on the ship abounded as to who we were, running from Hollywood's celebrities, etc. Seated to the Captain's right was the Director General of the United States State Department. After dinner was over the State Department official asked me what my connection was with the State Department. I told him I had just finished my assignment as the G.S.O. at Benghazi, Libya and was going on home leave.

Chapter Ten Our First Born and the Crown Prince

Chapter Eleven
The Supply Officer

Chapter Eleven The Supply Officer

As the ship approached the New York Harbor, arrangements were made for one departure from the vessel. The Purser told us our baggage would be handled by their personnel and that a vehicle had been provided by the shipping line and would be at the foot of the gangway to take us to our destination in Connecticut and we should go up to the bridge deck accordingly. A crew member escorted us to the departure location.

The Chief Purser put up his hand and blocked everyone departing the ship and said, "Mr. and Mrs. Hyder first." This added to our departure confusion.

My father and mother were in a limousine provided by the American Export Lines that took us to their home in Branford, Connecticut. This was the first time my parents had seen us since we were married and now had met their new grandchild, Mark Jay Hyder.

We had fun with our family all around us.

Sheila had three new sisters-in-law, all of whom kept her busy, especially my brother Richard's wife, Mary. We were enjoying our home leave and shopping in New York while Mary, my sister-in-law took care of our son, Mark.

On 10 March I went to Washington, D.C. to report in at the State Department. I was informed that my new post would be Kabul, Afghanistan; my assignment would be Supply Management Officer at the post. I was further told that I would attend the Foreign Service Institute (F.S.I.) In Washington, D.C. where I would study conditions at the post and study the Farsi language.

During my various assignments in the Middle East I had attended many conferences in which I had urged that the success of any economic project would require the availability of water. The ruins of old Greco-Roman aqueducts that provided water throughout the Middle East are still apparently in evidence today. I firmly believe that much of the political and economic difficulties that we face in the Middle East today could be overcome by the development of a new political and economic union between all of the countries of the area from Turkey through the Arabian Peninsula including Israel and Egypt.

If this cannot be successfully attained confrontations between each of these countries will continue. Perhaps one of the secrets to achieve such a union would be for Zionism to recognize that when the Lord told Moses that He would help him lead the Jewish nation to the Promised Land that He meant that all of the children of Abraham should come together to develop the Great Syrian Desert and make it productive in producing food

Chapter Eleven The Supply Officer

for all of the people.

We also had to arrange for Coca to visit the veterinarian for a health examination and shots for travel to Afghanistan. Within three days of receiving his injection of distemper vaccine, Coca went blind. Sheila and I were very upset and realized Coca had to be put to sleep prior to our international travel.

On 15 April we departed the United States from Dulles Airport headed for Afghanistan and while enroute stopped at Beirut, Lebanon for a week. We arrived at Kandahar International Airport. We visited Sheila's parents at Beirut, Lebanon. Sheila's father was upset that I was taking her and his grandchild into this remote area. I then learned that he had previously visited Kabul in 1943 at the request of President Roosevelt and was the first American envoy to Afghanistan. He was to contract and purchase the entire Karabul Fur Industry for firms in the United States. He shared some of his travel experiences and difficulties he had going from Peshawar to Kabul. At that time there was no paved road and they had to ford rivers. He said it took him three days to make the trip.

At Kandahar we were to travel to Kabul via the Royal Afghan Airlines, locally called the Inshala Airlines. We were soon to learn what this meant. The next day we boarded the airline for Kabul; it was a DC-3. We went to the departure runway while the pilot checked his engines and stated his takeoff. The plane was increasing speed as it went down the runway but never reached rotation speed and we went 100 feet beyond the runway.

He stopped, turned the plane around and returned to his starting point on the runway.

We next heard the pilot say, "We did not make it this time. Inshala, bukarah; we will make it next time."

We returned to the Staff House at Kandahar where we met the Ambassador's secretary who was returning to post. We told her about our unfortunate loss of Coca. She told us that her dog had accompanied her from Germany, had pups and had offered one to another secretary in Kabul. That secretary was unable to care for the dog and was looking for a new home. She wanted to know if we would be interested in getting that pup. We said yes immediately, and Mark had a new buddy. We named this new dog Malik, which in Arabic means "King."

The next day the pilot informed us there would be another day's delay since it had rained the previous day in Kabul.

The Kabul manager had tested the runway and said the ground would be too soft for a safe landing. I asked the pilot how the Kabul manager had made that determination.

He said, "We went out to the runway and stuck his finger in the ground, and if it went past his first knuckle, the airport would be closed for landing and Inshala, bukarah would be better." Anyway we made it the next day arriving at our new post in Kabul, Afghanistan.

We were put in the Embassy staff house at Kabul awaiting my assignment of housing. We spent two days looking at potential locations; none of them met our requirements because Sheila was now pregnant again, with a due date projected to be the 4th week of December 1959. The General Services Officer (G.S.O.) took us to a property located at an area called Carta-Char. I looked at the compound which included four acres with many fruit

Chapter Eleven The Supply Officer

trees and a long grape arbor.

I told the G.S.O. "I'll take it!"

He said, "Don't you want to see the house first?"

I replied, "I like the grounds and the trees and whatever the house needs, you can fix it."

When he insisted that I look at the house, I went with him. He showed me a house with the roof falling in.

He asked, "Do you want me to show you some other houses?" I said, "No, you can get it fixed to my requirements." This was done and we moved into our new house on 15 May 1959.

Among my duties were the logistics, and management of the "pipeline" from offshore resources for the USAID and American Embassy to destinations in Afghanistan. This also included trans-shipment points in Pakistan, Iran, and Russia.

I was also the Procurement and Contracting Officer of the mission. My job required considerable travel to various outlying posts in Pakistan, Iran, USSR, and India and extensive negotiations at border crossing points. I maintained a full time office located at the Peshawar Officers' Club that had originally been the British Officers' Club in the northwest Province of India.

In early 1959 we transported 50,000 tons of wheat from the United States designated for Afghanistan. This shipment was offloaded at the Port of Karachi and shipped by rail to the appropriate entry port at Peshawar, Pakistan. During this transshipment period the governments of Pakistan and Afghanistan had encountered a controversy which resulted in the closure of the border.

The 50,000 tons of wheat destined for Kabul had

reached the entry point at Peshawar into Afghanistan in July 1959 and was located at the end of the rail line in Pakistan. Due to the border closing we were unable to move it forward to Kabul and Afghanistan. After three months of heavy rain the wheat became wet and seriously damaged and was no longer edible.

In October the government of Pakistan wanted it moved from their territory and the Afghanistans refused because it was damaged goods.

My constant efforts to resolve the problem were unproductive.

With my constant travel and negotiations between the capitol of Pakistan and the capitol of Afghanistan, we arrived at an emergency acceptable solution. This required a temporary relocation of a section of the Afghan-Pakistan border for 10 days. On paper the Afghan border would be moved south into Pakistan to extend beyond the rotting 50,000 tons of wheat.

I arranged for a loan of road construction equipment located nearby from our contractor, Raymund Morrison-Knudson who was building the road from Kabul to Peshawar. Their first step was to hollow out a hole in the Aphgahan Desert nearby, large enough to receive all of the damaged wheat. They would then use large caterpillar bulldozers to push the damaged wheat out of Pakistan and into Afghanistan. Upon completion of the relocation of the damaged wheat, they would cover it over with sand from the Aphgahan Desert and level it off. Upon completion of this activity the Pack/Aphgan borders would be returned to their original position.

While I was supervising this logistic operation, the

Chapter Eleven The Supply Officer

American Counsel at Peshawar notified me that my wife Sheila was sitting on a large rock between the Afghan and Pakistan border checkpoints to the Khyber-Pass. My driver picked me up from our work site and took me to locate Sheila and render assistance. We found Sheila as reported, sitting calmly waiting for me.

When I arrived she looked up at me and said, "I'm so embarrassed."

I asked, "What happened?"

She handed me her passport. Upon examination I found the photograph was of a two-week old baby, i.e., our son, Mark. The Afghan border officials knew that Sheila was my wife and traveled often with me to Pakistan and let her go through the checkpoint. The Pakistan border officials asked Sheila if this was her passport. She said she made a mistake and had picked up the wrong passport. The Pakistan officials would not let her proceed. I told them not a problem. I took out my special passport, turned to a blank page. I wrote in Mrs. Sheila Hyder is accompanying her husband, Maurice J. Hyder, on official business of the United States, and signed the document. Sheila got into my car and we proceeded to the Pakistan checkpoint and handed my passport to the officials.

They looked at me and I asked, "Any difficulties?"

They hesitated and then said "Proceed." A week later, Sheila and I returned to Kabul.

In November 1959, Sheila traveled to Beirut, Lebanon where she was to give birth to our new baby. Our baby was expected to be born at the American University Hospital at Beirut. I was in constant communication with Sheila;

I had become concerned as her due date had already passed. I arranged for travel to go to Beirut to be with Sheila and would be accompanied by my son, Mark.

Located next to my office was a small communications room which contained communication to key points in Afghanistan where we had United States representatives. On the morning of 21 December I heard some excited outbursts from our representative at Kandahar. I rushed to the radio and wrote down what seemed to be developing emergency that was occurring at the post in Kandahar. I called our Executive Officer who in turn notified our Ambassador, Hank Byroade. Hank asked me to come to his office immediately. He asked me to report exactly what I had heard from the Kandahar Post involving our American representatives and Aphgan personnel.

After my explanation Hank picked up his phone and called the Prime Minister and asked him, "Is there anything going on at Kandahar?"

The Prime Minister said, "No, Mr. Ambassador, everything is fine there."

The Ambassador said, "Very good. Please notify the airport at Kandahar that I will be landing there within the hour to meet my people."

The Prime Minister said, "That won't be possible, Mr. Ambassador, because the landing strip to the airport is being repaired."

The Ambassador said, "Mr. Prime Minister, I'm leaving immediately for Kandahar in 30 minutes and if I run into any problem there the United States Air Force will be over Afghanistan within the hour! I know you are leaving for Beirut to see Sheila. I want you to hand carry the

Chapter Eleven The Supply Officer

diplomatic pouch in which I will include my report on this incident. You will put this personally into the hands of the Ambassador to Beirut when you arrive there."

Ambassador Byroade boarded his plane at Kabul, piloted by his United States Air Force Attaché'; upon arrival at Kandahar, he found that his representative was in the hospital with knife wounds, and other local personnel were also being treated there. He returned to Kabul and handed me classified documents in a diplomatic pouch which I was to hand carry to the American Ambassador in Beirut, Lebanon.

My son and I went to the Kabul Airport and boarded our flight to Beirut. Prior to our departure the flight steward said all passengers would have to leave the plane and would be placed on another flight. The steward stopped me and said my son and I would remain on board that aircraft.

Upon my inquiry, the steward told me that due to civil unrest all Afghans were restricted from departing the country. I found that Mark and I had an aircraft all to ourselves on our flight to Beirut. We arrived the morning of 24 December at the airport. At Customs and Immigration I was asked to open my bags for inspection. I had two bags, one of which was a Pan Am flight bag. I respectfully opened my suitcase and asked the official to not open the Pan Am bag as it would embarrass me. He ignored my wish and proceeded to open it. To his consternation he found it full of Mark's dirty diapers, and was embarrassed and told me to move on. I departed the airport in a taxi and went directly to the American Embassy in Beirut, and asked the Marine guard to take me to the Ambassador.

I told the Marine guard I had a special diplomatic punch which was to be personally handed to the Ambassador designated eyes only. This was accomplished.

While there I asked for directions to the A.U.B. Hospital. When I arrived at the hospital I asked if they knew where my wife Sheila was since she had already checked in. A young student nurse took us to an A.U.B. apartment nearby at 11:00 a.m.

I thanked the nurse and rang the door bell. Sheila opened the door and was surprised to see us. She was so excited, gave me a big hug and kiss, and did the same for her son. She offered me coffee and a donut as we sat holding hands and was full of questions.

About a half hour later she put her hands on her tummy, and said, "It's coming!"

I asked her "What?"

She said, "I'm in labor," handing me the phone and told me to call the doctor. When I reached the doctor she asked to talk to Sheila who explained her situation. She handed the phone to me and the doctor instructed me to bring Sheila to the hospital immediately.

The nurse who brought me here was instructed to stay with Mark and gave me directions to the maternity ward. Thirty minutes later the doctor told me to get out of the room; the baby was coming. The doctor told me that my arrival broke the dam, rushed Sheila into the delivery room. Fifteen minutes later I was told I could go in and meet my new son, Craig.

Chapter Eleven The Supply Officer

Chapter Twelve
Baby Chicks

Chapter Twelve Baby Chicks

I went into the delivery room, gave Sheila a big hug and kiss congratulating her on her fine performance. Sheila told me that my cousin Kamal Saad had invited her to a Christmas Eve party at their home and I should attend bearing great news. I picked up a box of cigars at the hospital store to take with me. I had a great time with my cousins who toasted the newborn very often during the evening.

Sheila, the two boys, and I returned to Kabul and celebrated our third wedding anniversary on 27 December. Many of our friends from the Embassy at Kabul called upon us to meet our new arrival and to share in our Christmas joy.

Sheila had previously asked me about raising some chickens so that she could have fresh eggs at Kabul. We obtained suggestions from our poultry advisor, Boyd Ivory, an L.D.S. technician of USAID.

He gave us suggestions of preparing a hen coop which would be built to the rear of our home around the outside base of the living room fireplace. The poultry advisor of our U.S. Mission brought over 50 baby chicks and she took great pleasure in watching them develop. The poultry advisor designed boxes on shelves in the coop which would become the hens' nests. Within the next several months the hens started to produce eggs and to Sheila's delight, the first eggs were all double-yolk and she gave eggs to our Embassy friends. Soon we were able to identify the roosters from the hens and the roosters were processed and put in our freezer, all except the one we named Chanticleer, a Rhode Island Red. He became our morning alarm getting me up at the crack of dawn without fail! About four weeks later Sheila reported to me that Chanticleer declared himself king of the coop and resented Sheila picking up eggs from his wives and would peck at her when she came into the coop. I spoke to our cook Baktiari who said Chanticleer had lost is head and therefore became dinner that week for dinner!

In the spring of 1960, the State Department sent me to Ohio State University to take a course in Logistics Management.

We returned to our post in Kabul in June of 1960. In July 1960, Sheila and I took the boys on a vacation in Kashmir, India. We rented a houseboat on Dahl Lake in the Vail of Kashmir.

The houseboat came with 3 bedrooms, bath, and two servants. Instead of going to market, the market came to our boat.

Two Kashmir boys paddled a large a canoe and sold us

Chapter Twelve Baby Chicks

fresh fruits and vegetables; this was a good experience for us. The entire setting reminded us of the movie "Shangri-La." After experiencing the beauty of Kashmir it was difficult to return to Kabul.

During the first week of September 1960, we took a trip to Bamian, a beautiful valley, a few hours drive north of Kabul. There we were awed at the magnificent Buddha carved into the red mountain. The Buddha was approximately 150 feet high and 80 feet wide. It was a Buddhist temple. The Buddhist monks lived in caves carved into the mountain to the sides and rear of the statue. Sheila and I took the opportunity to climb up the stairs to visit the monks and came back down; it was a very rewarding experience for us. It was a few years later that we learned that this Buddhist shrine statue was blown up by al-Qaeda terrorists.

This was a great tragedy to the world to lose one of the great wonders in Afghanistan.

In the middle of October, Sheila, the boys, and I took a camping trip to the Kings Valley (The Arger Valley) north of Benin. The King had given us a written invitation to visit his valley which provided fantastic trout fishing. When we arrived at the valley we found that the beautiful Kings Chalet located there. This staff of the Chalet approached us and told us our rooms at the chalet were ready for us. I told them that I was very thankful of the offer but we wanted to camp by the trout stream. We found a great location nearby and looked forward to our weekend fishing trip. We were going to rough it!

We had a land rover for transportation, a motor mechanic driver, a cook Bakiari, and our houseboy.

The next morning I stepped down into the stream, made my first cast and within two minutes had a three pound German brown trout! I called to Sheila to join me.

She said, "You're crazy waking me up this early!"

But she did get dressed and joined me stepping into the stream and we soon had a dozen fish between us. We gave the fish to our cook who prepared them for our breakfast.

About an hour after breakfast, three of the King's servants came down from the Chalet carrying 30 foot wide trays over their heads with fresh fruit and vegetables. This was the highlight of our camping trip. Sheila confided in me that she was pregnant and would have to check in with the doctor when we got home.

The baby was due in early May 1961. In the first week of November 1960 a message was sent to the State Department requesting permission to evacuate Sheila to an improved nearby location where she would give birth. Sheila would be attended to by a Seven Day Adventist, wife and husband medical team, through her pregnancy.

In January 1961 the Ambassador had been advised by the doctors that Sheila may encounter complications with her pregnancy and he had notified the United States State Department accordingly. The State Department had recommended that a medical clinic be built at Kabul to provide primary medical care. The Ambassador acknowledged the State Department reply and that he would keep them informed.

In mid-February 1961, Sheila came down with hepatitis, and the doctors became concerned and alerted me to possible complications.

At the request of the Ambassador I was to plan for a

Chapter Twelve Baby Chicks

new medical clinic building to be built and equipped to provide primary medical aid care in Kabul. This would be located at the Embassy compound. Construction would start in June 1960.

In early February 1961 the doctor advised Sheila that she might face some difficulty due to an RH complication and she would have to be monitored closely.

The projected date for opening the clinic was 1 April 1961. The doctor told me that Sheila would deliver closer to 10 April and they were monitoring her very carefully.

The doctor sent me out of the house to attend an Embassy activity at the Embassy Compound staff house. While there I received a call from the doctor saying that due to an RH complication Sharon was failing and needed an immediate blood transfusion. I notified everyone in attendance and told them of our need for a RH negative blood. We had two volunteers.

The first blood donor was the Protestant pastor who had been drinking cocktails at the party in Kabul, and Sharon's system rejected his blood. We encountered complications since a required two-way valve to manage the transfusion was unavailable. The transfusion was carried out with a new donor, a 20-year-old blonde, blue-eyed, and freckled girl who had recently arrived at the Embassy from the Midwest. Sharon responded well to her blood. The doctors took one hyperemic withdrawal from the donor and put it into Sharon and then withdrew a similar amount from Sharon; this continued for an hour. The doctors did not expect Sharon to survive and the Paple representative from the Italian Embassy gave Sharon her last rites from the Catholic Church. In the meantime, all of the participants from the Embassy party had gathered outside where the drama was taking place, holding a prayer vigil for Sharon. The Lord was with us and Sharon survived. Historically, this was the first successful infant transfusion in Afghanistan. Sharon was baptized by the Papl-Nuncio of the Italian Embassy.

The American Ambassador, Hank Byroade, and his wife Mary, were the volunteer Godparents.

I organized Boy Scouts of America troop at the American Embassy. American community boys between 10-20 years old became members. In May 1962 we also opened the troops to local and other Afghan boys of the Diplomatic community.

Our outdoor activities included hiking and overnight camping in the nearby mountains and valleys. One of our weekend camping trips was at the Buddhist Park at Bamine. Our meeting place was at the United States staff house at the Embassy compound in Kabul. It was a popular activity for the boys.

A Girl Scout troop had also been organized and my wife, Sheila was one of the leaders. I also worked with Afghan teachers who organized two Afghan Boy Scout troops. Our troops interacted with them and we were able to provide scout handbooks and equipment for our Afghan friends.

In 1962 the border between Afghanistan and Pakistan was closed again and we encountered difficulties in the movement of our supply requirements since Afghanistan was a landlocked country. We received offers of assistance from Russia and Iran to utilize these countries for our re-supply pipeline.

Chapter Twelve Baby Chicks

Our Ambassador sent me in February 1963 on a fact-finding mission to Pakistan, India, Iran, and Russia to obtain cost analysis of the available transportation from potential arrival and trans-shipment ports to Kabul.

I reported my findings to Ambassador Byroade and made recommendations based upon my logistic study. He was under pressure from the King's Prime Minister (P.M.) Amieen who wanted the United States to support building and development of a new seaport at Bandar Abbas on the Persian Gulf. The Afghan P.M. also wanted the United States to build a railroad from Bandar Abbas to Kabul, through the Afghan Province of Balustan. I told the Ambassador that the project cost requested by the Prime Minister Amieen would be prohibitive. I recommended that every effort should be made to reopen the pipeline from Karachi to Kabul via Phesawar and Kandahar. The Ambassador concurred and said he would arrange a meeting with King Zhair-Kahn and wanted me to attend the meeting.

He called me three days later and to bring all my surveys, records, and recommendations and join him. We went to the King's palace for the meeting. P.M. Ameen also attended. Ambassador Byroade summarized my report and the United States' recommendation to the King. P.M. Ameen objected and said he did not want to use Karachi and that the shipping route through Iran was more economical. At this juncture the Ambassador told me to make my presentation to the King using my supporting documents.

I did so and told the King based on the study that the cost to the United States would be more than double for a logistics route through Khaomshar, Iran. Shipping time through Iran to Kabul would be more than double. I recommended that Afghanistan reopen negotiations with Pakistan so that the shipping route from Karachi to Kabul could be used.

The P.M. Ameen stood up and told the King, "If you are going to listen to Mr. Hyder, I'm going to resign."

The King looked up and said, "Mr. Prime Minister, I accept your resignation."

After P.M. Ameen departed, the King told the Ambassador he would follow the Ambassador's recommendations. He also asked that the American Ambassador to Pakistan assist in the negotiations.

Two hours after I got home a vehicle from the Embassy handed me a note from the Ambassador. He instructed me to immediately bring my family to the Embassy for our safety. This we did. I was told after I arrived that the Prime Minister of Afghanistan had put a contract out to kill me. Within 10 days the border between Pakistan and Afghanistan was reopened and travel and shipments returned to normal.

Chapter Twelve Baby Chicks

Chapter Thirteen
Off to Viet Nam

CHAPTER THIRTEEN OFF TO VIET NAM

In October 1963 I received an offer of a direct transfer from Afghanistan to Vietnam. We packed up our household and personal items and traveled to New Delhi, India and onward to Saigon, Vietnam via Calcutta and Bangkok. We arrived at Saigon Airport at 2:00 p.m. on 9 October 1963.

There was no one there to meet us so I called the American Embassy for instructions. They asked me where I was calling from because they had sent many cables to stop our forward travel at New Delhi and Calcutta. I told them I was at the Saigon Airport. The United States Embassy informed me that the country was in the middle of a coup and that all local travel was dangerous. They said they would try to arrange a vehicle to be sent and pick us up and take us to a United States staff house in Saigon. We were taken to the Nor Odom Embassy Staff house which was designated to be the new site of the American Embassy. I was later to learn that when we landed at the south side of the airport, that a United States Naval Field Hospital had arrived and been set up at the north side of the airport.

My close friend, Bill Ferris, was in charge of that field hospital. When we arrived at the Nor Odom staff house, I could hear increasing gun fire nearby. I told my wife and children to get under the bed and keep their heads down and I joined them. After the gunfire stopped we came out from under the bed. We found incoming holes on one side of the wall and outgoing holes on the opposite side. We found more than a dozen pieces of shrapnel on top of the bed we were under.

The next morning we were told that President Diem and Madam Nhu had been killed the day before, and that Vietnam had a new government. A few days later we were assigned to our new residence in a compound adjacent to the Saigon airport Tan-Son-Nhut. My children attended a Vietnamese elementary school and I acquired a used Oldsmobile 98 Sedan from a retiring Embassy official. I hired a Vietnamese driver for that vehicle. My children weekly attended the United States Military Theater in downtown Saigon called "The Captain Kindo Theatre." In late October 1963, a Viet Cong terrorist threw a bomb in The Captain Kindo Theatre causing many causalities. My children escaped with a few splinters and I was thankful. They did not attend the theatre again.

On 30 October while Sheila and the children were attending a baseball game near the airport, a Viet Cong threw a bomb into the bleachers. Sheila and the children were not hurt, but this was the second incident to occur and increased my concern for them.

I decided to send them home as soon as possible for their safety and my peace of mind. I sent a cable to Sheila's parents and asked them to meet them upon their arrival

Chapter Thirteen Off to Viet Nam

Charles Bunker

Manton Mauvricks

at Travis Air Force Base in Fairfield County, California. I suggested to them they bring warm clothing and blankets for the members of my family since they would be arriving from Vietnam without any warm clothing. I was notified that everything went well and my family was now at Mi-Wuk Village, California.

I corresponded with Sheila and told her I would be coming on home leave to Mi-Wuk in February 1964, and was looking forward to being with my family.

My assignment at USAID, Vietnam, was as chief of and director of Procurement the Logistics there. My office staff included 05 and 06 active military personnel and retired military personnel. I was also surprised to find my new 06 Navy Captain who had been my skipper on the USS Duluth had arrived as a new staff member. My staff was preparing a logistic study on South Vietnam. We were determining the condition of roads, bridges, and ports in Vietnam. We were also updating navigational charts of Cam-Renh Bay on the east coast of Vietnam as well as the ports of Saigon, Nha Trang, and Da Nang. We had also established provincial supply warehouses in support of the provinces in South Vietnam and the United States Military Command Vietnam (MAC-V). We also developed a military supply and logistics manual in Vietnamese and English to standardize supply practices in Vietnam. I had to make personal inspections of our activities at each Province once a month. I was also very fortunate to have retired military. World War II Japanese American Nisei and Tansies sergeants were assigned to my staff.

In 1964 when we were on home leave at Mi-Wok, my

Chapter Thirteen Off to Viet Nam

mother-in-law, Helen Bunker-Howard, told me some of the interesting facts that occurred just prior to Sheila's birth. She told me that her uncle Manton Maurick had been the founder of the Continental Casualty Insurance Company which was by that time a billion dollar corporation. He had told Helen that when her child was born it would be Manton Maurick's first great-grandniece or nephew and he would like to set up a multimillion dollar trust for that child. He insisted the name of the new child should include the name Mauvrick as the name of the child to receive the financial gift. That new child born to Helen was my wife, Sheila. Helen told Manton Maurick that she could not saddle Sheila as requested since that would make her name Sheila Maurick Howard and consequently, the financial gift never was made. A few months later Manton's first grandnephew was born in Toronto, Canada and his name became George Maurick Bunker along with some partners founded the Martin-Murietta Corporation which as the primary supplier of military assistance to the United States military effort in Vietnam. Sheila and I hosted George Bunker and his wife at our home in Washington, D.C. By that time he was a multi-millionaire during the Vietnam War.

On one such occasion while traveling in the Montanrad Yard Province, my jeep driven by Major Wayne Allen, was blown up when we drove over a land mine. We were not wounded since we had removed the seat and had replaced them with sandbags to protect us.

My other means of transportation to the other Provinces was by air. We employed the use of a Porter Aircraft which was one-third (1/3rd) engine and had space only for the pilot and co-pilot; I flew as co-pilot.

The passenger's compartments were protected by steel plates capable of stopping rifle bullets. The Porter was capable of taking off and landing within 100 feet to reduce our exposure to enemy fire. While I was in the North Province off Vietnam I was exposed to Agent Orange.

After we completed the logistics study of roads, bridges, and ports of Vietnam, I ran into difficulties in getting my logistics study published. I required 50 copies. I did not have enough money in my budget to provide for this. This was the spring of 1965. One of my staffers, Colonel (Col.) Rusty Blankenship an 06, told me he had met with Brigadier General (Brig.Gen.) Frank Osmanski; he was the J-4 of MACV, who offered to print the study. Little did I know the part I would play in upcoming United States Military escalation in South Vietnam. I asked Col. Blankenship to obtain 50 copies of our study from Military Assistance Command in Vietnam (MAC-V), the escalated military action in Vietnam followed. Blankenship told me that Gen. Osmanski had reclassified our study as "TOP SECRET" and refused to release any copies to me. I called Gen. Osmanski and told him that my staff done the research and completed the drafted logistics study which was in our possession. He said, "I am General Osmanski and I am refusing to release that document." I told him, "I am MR. HYDER and outrank you, Sir. Please remember our President is called Mr. President!"

I had immediately reported our interchange to the United States Ambassador who laughed and told me he would take care of it. A few hours later Gen. Osmanski called my office and asked for Col. Blankenship to report

CHAPTER THIRTEEN OFF TO VIET NAM

to him. We turned over our 50 copies to Col. Blankenship by one of my staff officers. Our study was used by the United States military in the escalating conflict.

Some weeks later the Tonkin Gulf incident occurred. President Johnson stated that North Korea had attacked a United States destroyer in the Tonkin Gulf in the South China Sea. United States military action escalated against military action against North Vietnam.

Chapter Fourteen
Back Stateside

Chapter Fourteen Back Stateside

In 1966 I received orders transferring me from Saigon to the United States Department of State. Vietnam logistics did a temporary assignment at San Francisco. After reviewing my transfer orders I contacted my back stop office in Washington and requested a temporary assignment at San Francisco. My orders were changed to comply with my request. I received a temporary assignment to Region 9 G.S.A., San Francisco. We located a rental at Hayward, California and I communicated daily to the United States Government Building in San Francisco. I had agreed with the director of Region 9 to do an End Use Audit of G.S.A. activities which covered most of the Western United States of America.

He insisted that all of my findings would be reported only to him.

He was upset when I reported that his Office of Procurement had been paying $500.00 for a ball peen hammer. This fact had been leaked from somebody in the G.S.A. to the press and caused public criticism.

There were many another issues that I reported to him which the director handled within his department. During the time I was in the San Francisco Bay area, I had become a staff member of the San Francisco Bay area Boy Scout's Council, B.S.A. I also became Scout Master of the troop located in Hayward, California. I arranged for a one week TDY to Washington, D.C. that my wife, Sheila and I could locate our future home in the D.C. area.

We bought a house in Vienna, Virginia in anticipation of our next move to the State Department in Washington, D.C.

When we arrived in California, we had bought a Pontiac station wagon and a Coleman Tent trailer and became gypsies.

At the end of June 1967, my family and I left Hayward, California touring north. We visited Mt. Lassen Volcano Park, Glen Burney Falls, and Mt. Shasta. We traveled north to the Olympic Peninsula and crossed over to Victoria Island where we visited the beautiful parks and gardens located there. Then we went by ferry to British Columbia and traveled east.

We visited Glacier National Park, Custer Battle Field, and Mt. Rushmore. Then we went eastward through Canada to attend 1967 Montreal, Canada World Fair. We took this opportunity to visit Toronto, Canada where we visited Sheila's great aunt and cousins in the Bunker family. We then traveled south through Maine and New

Chapter Fourteen Back Stateside

England and arrived at our new home in Vienna, Virginia arriving 10 July. Our long time friends, the Doyles family who lived nearby in Falls Church, Virginia.

I left my Pontiac with Sheila for her family duties with children and shopping. I purchased a small Italian Fiat vehicle through my diplomatic entitlement. I used this vehicle for my daily commute to the State Department.

Upon my arrival at Vienna, word had preceded me and I found out that the National Capital Area Council (N.C.A.C.) had appointed me as District Commissioner of the Fairfax Co-Council BSA. I was invited by the National Capitol Area (N.C.A.C.) Council to participate in the upcoming Wood Bridge training course. I accepted. When all of the training participant had arrived at the training course site, I found that I had been appointed to the Bear Patrol.

Following the completion of training program, I was required to complete a ticket as determined by my advisor before receiving my award.

One of the major activities that I had accomplished as District Commissioner was arranging for a historic 3-day camporee at Yorktown, Virginia. We had 2,500 participants. During the second day of the camporee, my commissioner staff had encountered a difficult situation and called my attention to the problem. Two young scouts were found in their tents comatose. Upon examination by our medical staff, they were found drunk. Since they were only 12 years old, I determined they were in a dangerous condition; I called the highway patrol who arranged for an ambulance to take them to the local hospital where they were treated and recovered. I further had their Scout master call their parents to come to the encampment and take their sons home. My responsibilities as District Commissioner prepared me for handling many similar major events in the future.

While I was sent to Washington to update my knowledge of procedures and policies, I had been assigned to the Vietnam desk as the Logistics Specialist for Vietnam. This assignment was to last approximately five years at this point. When I reported to my new supervisor at the Vietnam desk, I was confronted by my old friend, Brig. Gen. Frank Osmanski who had retired from the Army and had been hired by the State Department and had now become my boss. Under the circumstances, I suggested that he might want me to be re-assigned to another office.

He said, "That if I could carry out my job as I did in Vietnam, he wanted me on his team." We became very good friends and his wife and Sheila hit it off.

In October 1967 Frank and I were sent to Vietnam on an inspection tour to review effectiveness and response of the supply situation. In March 1968 a document crossed my desk requesting a logistics officer to go to Rio de Janeiro, Brazil. Since I had met all of the requirements stipulated for that position. I called Sheila and asked her if she'd like to go to Brazil.

She responded, "Yes, are we getting a transfer?"

I responded, "No, but the post is looking for someone with my qualifications."

I entered my name as a prospective replacement for Brazil, signed the document, and forwarded it for endorsement. Each supervisor, including Osmanski and the Secretary of State approved it and I received my transfer.

Chapter Fourteen Back Stateside

As I was clearing my desk, Osmanski asked me what I was doing. I told him I had been transferred to Brazil.

He said, "Who approved that? You are supposed to be here for a minimum of five years!"

I replied, "You did!"

Chapter Fifteen
Ipanema beach and the Boy Scouts

Chapter Fifteen Ipanema beach and the Boy Scouts

I sold my Fiat to a colleague and got full payment for my car. A few weeks later we closed our home in Vienna, and left for Brazil. We arrived in Rio de Janeiro, Brazil at the beginning of Car-Ni-Val (carnival). Our temporary residence was an apartment near Ipa-Nema-Beach, Brazil.

In compliance to standard procedures, I reported to the Ambassador and submitted my orders. He welcomed me and I was surprised when he said before you undertake the duties of your office, there is somethin g else I want you to do. My office received a request from a SR Government official, whom we have be4en trying to befriend without much success. He said that he had received a notice from the B.S.A., N.C.A.C. advising the Brazilian PBS that one of their senior commissioners had been assigned to the American Embassy at Rio de Janeiro and that he would like to meet me.

His name was Oscar Olivera; he was Chancellor of the Universities of Brazil. He told me my first assignment at the Embassy was to contact Mr. Olivera and render any assistance we could offer to enlist his support. He handed me Mr. Oliver's calling card with his telephone number.

When I reached him, he invited me to lunch the next day.

I was to learn that his interest in me was due to a communication received by him from the National Council, B.S.A./N.C.A.C. After our luncheon Mr. Olivera introduced himself as the Chief Scout of the Boy Scouts of Brazil (B.S.B.). He explained that the Brazilian scouting movement was expanding and that they had been using the British Scouting handbook in their program. His goal was to develop a Brazilian scouting manual and asked my advice as to how they could accomplish that. I told him that this was an ambitious project but achievable.

I suggested that four educated young executives should be sent to the B.S.A. University of Scouting in New Jersey. They would develop an outline and prepare a syllabus for the Brazilian Scouting handbook. This would be prepared in the Brazilian language. I estimated it would take approximately four months to accomplish this when completed and approved by the Brazilian senior staff, the project would be approved for the publishing of the new handbook.

Mr. Olivera questioned, "Is that possible?" I told him, "Yes, but it would need the approval of the United States Ambassador," and suggested a conference at the United States Embassy between representatives of the B.S.B. and the American Embassy.

I reported back to the Ambassador that I had carried out his instruction and that a conference at the American Embassy should take place as soon as possible. He asked me what would be the approximate cost of the total project. I recommended a budget of approximately $78,000.00 to $80,000.00. I said that the success of this project would reach all of the youth in Brazil and would be part of the

Chapter Fifteen Ipanema beach and the Boy Scouts

B.S.B. movement in Brazilian schools.

Following approval of the project by the United States Ambassador, I submitted the project to the International Commissioner of the National Council B.S.A. Everyone agreed and four young B.S.B. executives were sent to the United States of America and spent four months preparing the syllabus of the new B.S.B. handbook.

Oscar Olivera approved of the handbook and it was printed. Two weeks after I had arrived in Brazil, the National Council B.S.A. had sent my approved certificate of Wood Badge completion to the B.S.B. It was awarded to me in the presence of the United States Ambassador by the Wood Badge Scout Master of Brazilian scouting, Jose Brito. I also became Scout Master of the American Embassy B.S.A. Boy Scout troop. The American Embassy authorized a new title for me as Scouting Attaché of Embassy. I also became a member of the B.S.B. Executive Board.

In the fall of 1968 I also attended the Jamboree Pan-Americano of Asuncion, Paraguay, as co-director of the B.S.B. Delegation. We paid our entrance fees and had set up our tents. An hour later I was approached by the driver of the American Ambassador at Asuncion, telling me the Ambassador would like to see me and my wife, Sheila.

The driver took us to the Ambassador at Asuncion. He asked us if we were still registered with the B.S.A. and the Girl Scouts of American (G.S.A.).

On being assured that we were, he told me to return to the Jamboree site and check in representing the B.S.A. and G.S.A. He told us too that the United States B.S.A. and G.S.A. delegation who had been enroute from the United States were stopped at Panama and turned back as a result of political conflict. He said that he had registered the B.S.A. and G.S.A. at the Jamboree site. Our sons, Mark and Craig, would be responsible in raising and lowering the American and B.S.A. flags. Sheila and our daughter Sharon would become responsible for daily raising and lowering the American and G.S.A. flags. We returned to the Jamboree site and re-registered as the B.S.A. and G.S.A. delegations paying our fees a second time.

Chapter Fifteen Ipanema beach and the Boy Scouts

LIFE GALLERY

Life Gallery

These few photographs represent the journey my life has taken me. Some names I can remember, and some not. Each are highlights of many of the world events I was privileged to expeirience.

All are part of the graciousness of our creator. He had a plan for me and gave me the abilities to complete each and every task I was handed.

Doran Hodge 1944 AGC

Maurice Always Smiling

CUBA

GTMO City Cuba

Life Gallery

AGC 1943

Paint Locker Buddies

AGC 1944

Life Gallery

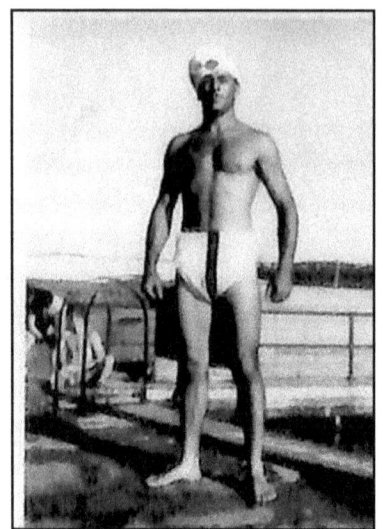

Buff Maurice

Maurice with pipe

Gunners Mate Annual

Gunners Mate

With the Gang for dinner

LIFE GALLERY

New York 1943

NEW YORK

HAWAII

Pearl Harbor

The Guys.

Life Gallery

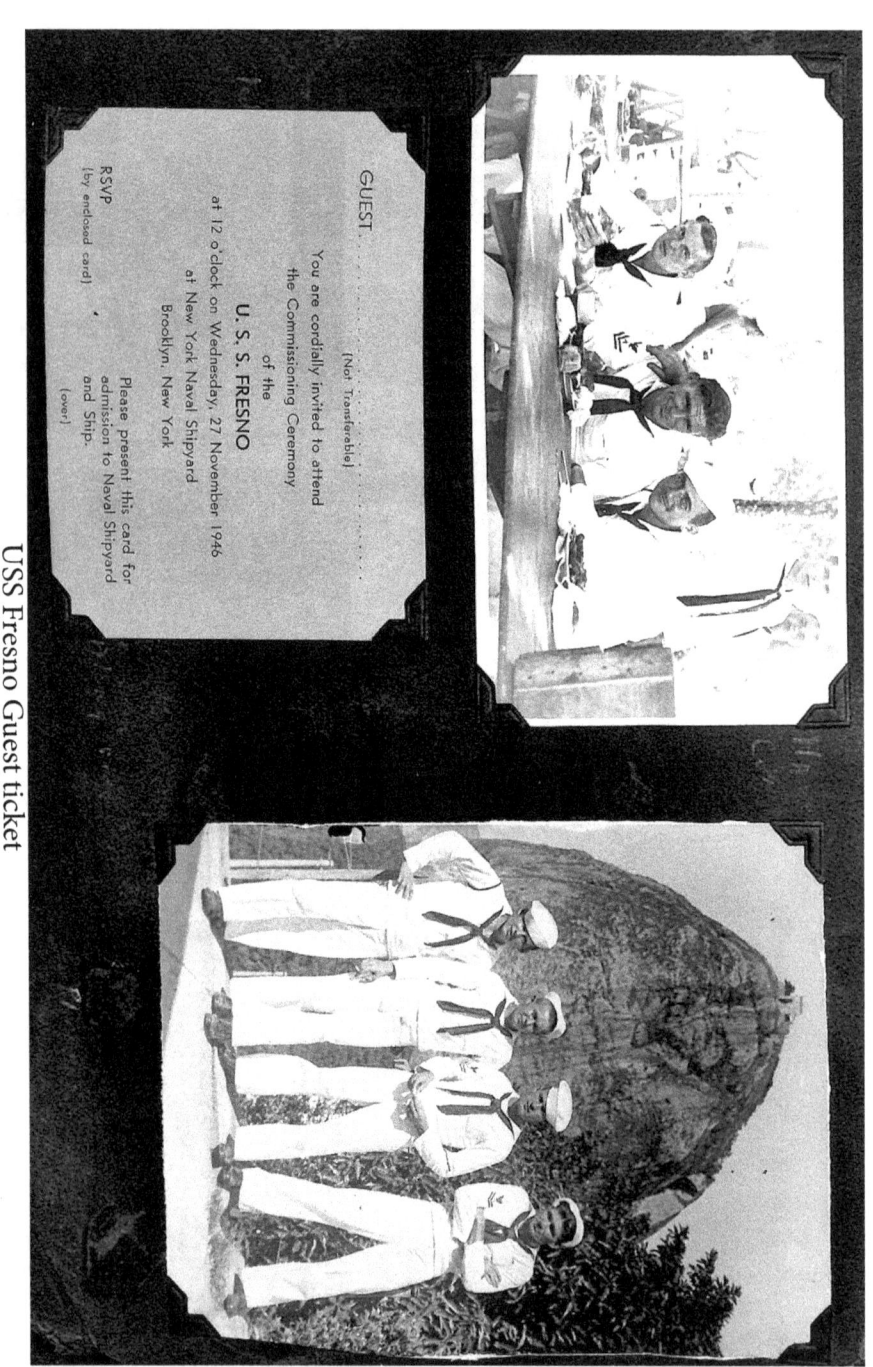

USS Fresno Guest ticket

Dottie

Sherman

To Maurice,
 I shall remember you always as a very dear person.
Most Sincerely,
Phyllis

Phyllis to Maurice

LIFE GALLERY

My Wonderful Amazing Beautiful Life

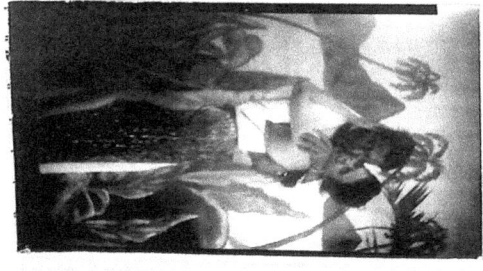

Maurice's adventures in the U.S. Navy

LIFE GALLERY

Shore Patrol Duty

HYDER MAURICE J
.....**USS WILLIAMS (DD-108) 1939**
.....**USS EAGLE (#19) 39/40**
.....**USS DUBUQUE 40/41**
.....**S.S.EXETER 41**
.....**M/V SATURNIA 42**
.....**S.S.EDWARD LUCKENBACH *7/2/42**
.....**S.S.HANNIBAL HAMLIN +43**
.....**USS DULUTH (CL-87) +44**
.....**USS FRESNO (CL-121) 45/46**
.....**USS JOHN WEEKS 47**

The Middle East

A Middle Eastern Beirut Temple Ruin

American University Beirut Sheila's Almamoter

LIFE GALLERY

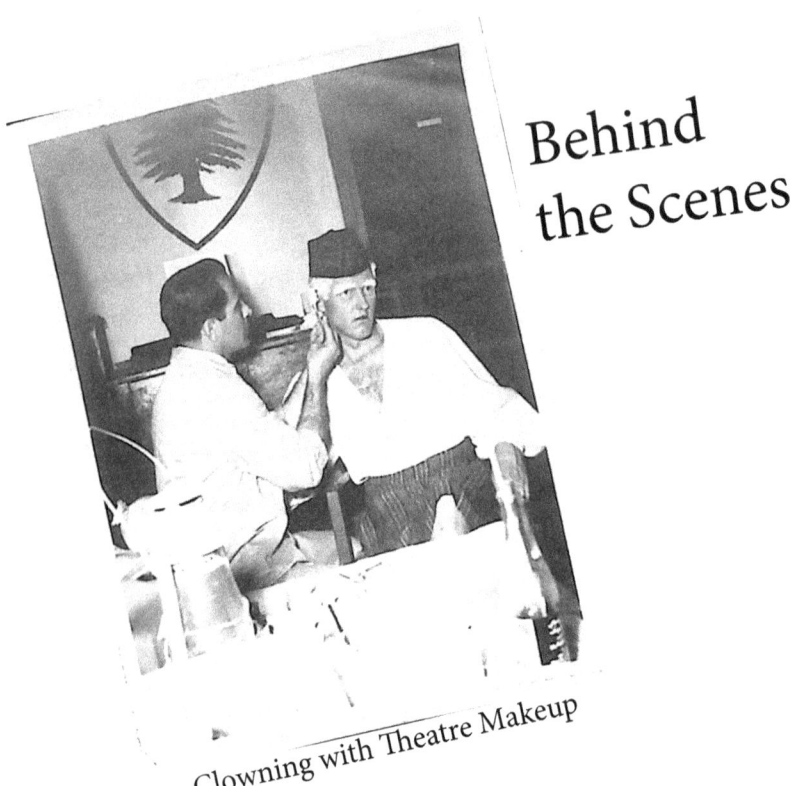

Behind the Scenes

Clowning with Theatre Makeup

The Student

Maurice Hyder

Cedars of Lebanon

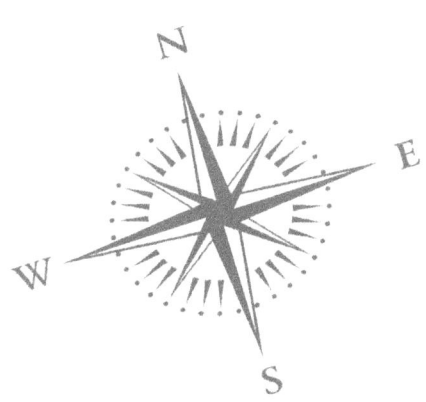

LIFE GALLERY

The Phillipines

Helping to feed the Phillipines 1970

My Wonderful Amazing Beautiful Life

Off Loading Bulgar Wheat in Phillipiness 1970

The Hyder Family

Mark J Hyder ..... Left

Sheila H. Hyder .... Back Row

Sharon Hyder..... Front Row center

Craig Hyder.... Right Front Row

Maurice J. Hyder.... Back Row Right

The Hyder Family

Starting at Right Top- Mark, Drew, Craig.

Right Center- Emily, Susan, Maurice, Jamie, Little Jamie

Bottom Row- Elizabeth, Sean, Mark

(Missing are Melissa, and Sharon)

Life Gallery

Mark, Sean, Emily, Melissa, Jaime, Elizabeth, Maurice

The Boy Scouts

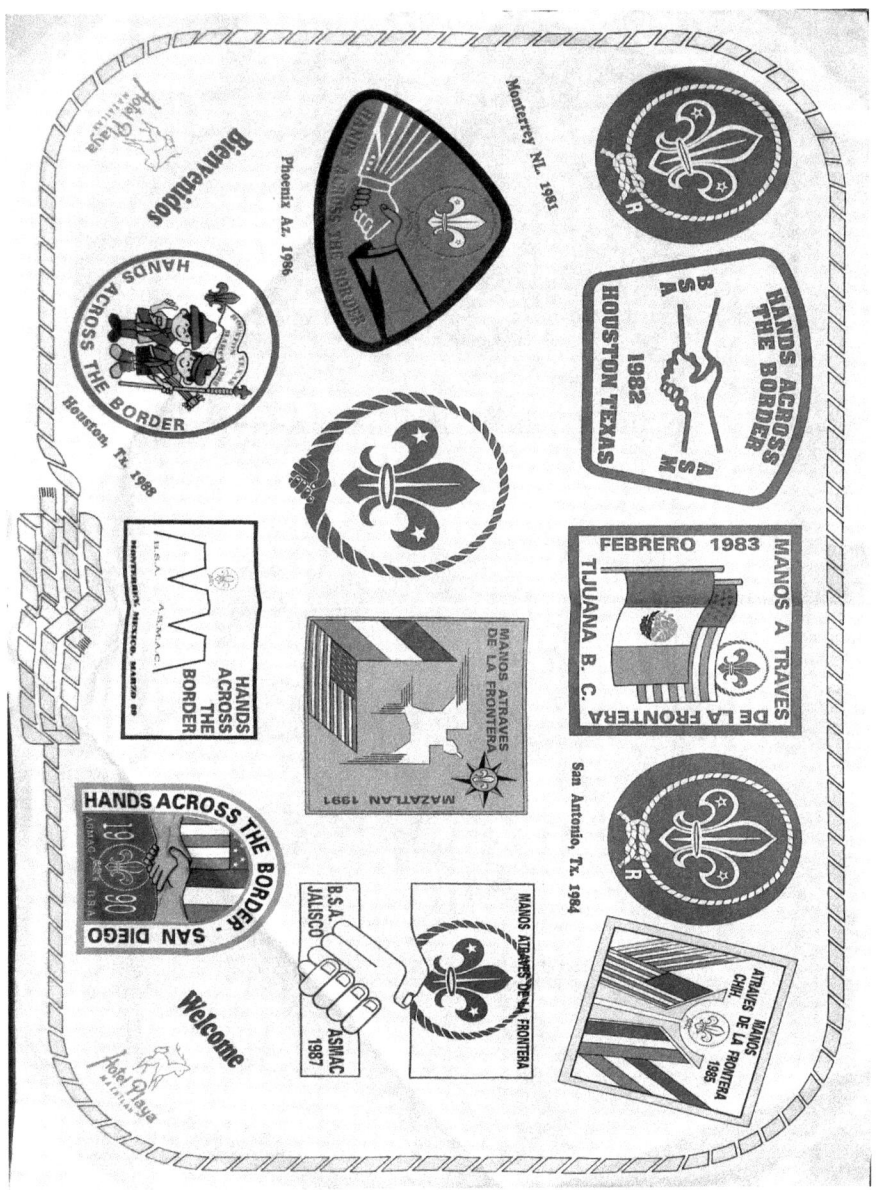

Life Gallery

National Council The Phillipines 1974

Taking the Oath of the BSA

Maurice in BSA Uniform

Maurice with Dog

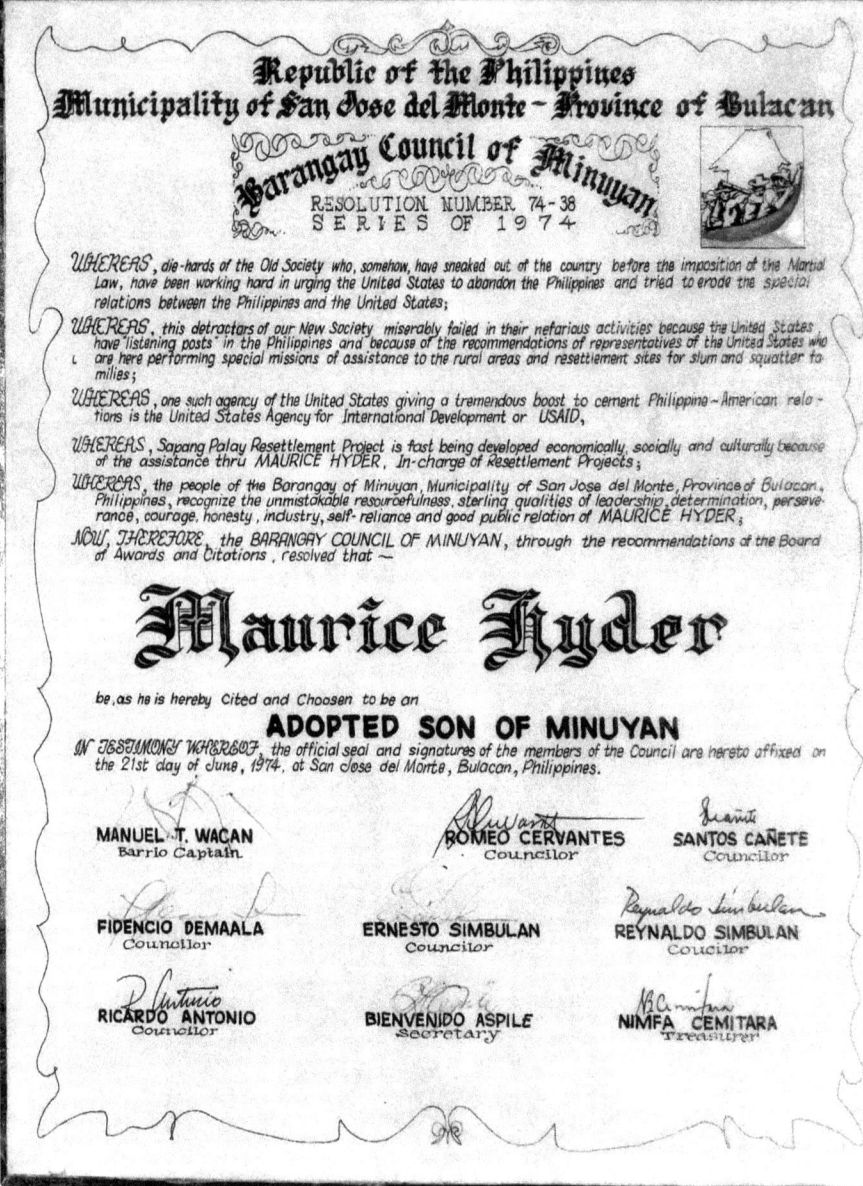

Republic of the Phillipines Proclomation 1974

Council Commissioner Uniform Looking Official

Life Gallery

The Boy Scouts of America
Emblem

Chapter Sixteen
One Ton of Beer

Chapter Sixteen One Ton of Beer

At the end of the Jamboree activity and closing camp fire, the Chief Scout of Paraguay presented us with their recognition of our attendance. It is my understanding that the 1968 Jamboree Pan-Americano attendance recognition was rejected by the B.S.A. since the formal delegation never arrived at Paraguay. The plaque now resides in a scouting museum in Kansas City, Kansas.

In the early spring of 1970 I received the B.S.B. National recognition at their National Court of Honor.

Sheila and I attended carnival 1970 and following the final ball arrived home late and was soon sound asleep.

At 6:00 a.m. we were awakened by the Ambassador driver who told me that the Ambassador had received a special message from the State Department concerning me and needed me at the Embassy immediately. I dressed quickly and went with the driver to the Embassy. At 6:30 a.m. I met with the Ambassador who showed me an urgent cable from the Secretary of state, Washington,

D.C. ordering me to Nigeria involving a very urgent matter. I told the Ambassador that I was involved in delicate negotiations at that time and suggested that since I had no special knowledge of Nigeria, perhaps another officer currently at the State Department could take the Nigerian assignment.

Within 15 minutes after sending our reply to the Secretary of State we received back a FLASH message to the American Ambassador stating that "Hyder will be on KLM flight at 11:00 a.m. that day or he was out of the agency!" With no further recourse, I returned home, told Sheila what had just transpired. I would have to go to Nigeria and would keep her informed of my whereabouts.

I took the KLM flight from Rio de Janeiro to Dakar, Senegal. When I arrived at Dakar, Senegal, I was met by the Nigerian and American Consuls who stamped visas in my passport. Then I was off to Lagos, Nigeria to find out what awaited me.

I arrived the next morning at 10:00 a.m. at the airport at Lagos, Nigeria, expecting a delegation to meet me in view of the pressure to get me to Nigeria. An American Embassy car and driver came out on the field and approached the plane. The driver asked me if I was Mr. Hyder to which I replied, "Yes" and he said, "We must leave immediately for the Embassy." I told him "I have to get my baggage." He told me his instructions were that I was to leave my baggage at the airport and was to report immediately to the Ambassador at the Embassy.

Upon arrival at the Embassy the Marine guard inquired whether I was Mr. Hyder and after acknowledgement was

Chapter Sixteen One Ton of Beer

told the Ambassador was waiting for me in the conference room and took me directly there. When I stepped into the room, the Ambassador walked around me saying,

"So you are Mr. Hyder who is going to solve our difficulties." I asked the Ambassador what was the difficulty that I was expected to handle and would he brief me accordingly. He told me that there had been a recent civil war in Nigeria involving the attempted breakaway of the Biafra Province. He said, "The Nigerian military forces under the command of Gen. Gowan, the President of Nigeria, had defeated the forces of Biafra. He told me that the American representatives in Nigeria had aided and abetted the Biafra rebels. Consequently, the Nigerian Government had declared that all American diplomatic and Embassy personnel had been declared persona-non-grata and were to remain in their homes. I then asked the Ambassador how he proposed that I could accomplish this. He said he didn't know but the Secretary of State had sent me to overcome the difficulty. Your assignment, Mr. Hyder, is to remove our persona-non-grata status in Nigeria.

I replied, "How am I supposed to do that?"

He replied, "I don't know but the President of the United States and the Secretary of State has submitted your name as an acceptable negotiator to resolve this difficulty."

I asked the Ambassador if he could give me some guidance and the parameters of my assignment.

He again looked at me in frustration and said, "You have already been told that and if you screw up, you are out of the agency!"

I shook my head in bewilderment and asked what resources were at my disposal.

He said, "You have a flight of 10 helicopters already loaded at the airport and the chief pilot is there awaiting your orders." He shook my hand and said, "Good luck" and I departed for the airport.

I met with the chief pilot who told me he had gotten clearance from the airport to head southeast to Engunu, Biafra. We arrived at the airport at approximately 12:30 a.m.

Upon arrival at Engunu, landing at the airport a platoon of Nigerian military ordered all of the pilots to leave their aircrafts and get down on their stomachs. They proceeded remove wallets, wrist watches, jewelry, etc. While I was lying on the ground I could feel blood dripping from my neck where a soldier had stuck the tip of his bayonet, breaking my skin.

My anger escalated. I reached up with my right hand, grabbed the bayonet, pushed it to one side, and said, "I want to see your officer in command immediately. I am here under direct orders of our President, General Gowan."

That appeared to be the magic word. I told him that I have arrived in Nigeria from Brazil in South America in compliance with a request from your government and did not expect to be received and treated in the manner I have just experienced at your airport. I further told him that his military people were to return all the personal property removed from my pilots and not to be harmed further. The Captain complied. I asked him to take me to the Commanding Officer of this military area. I told the

Chapter Sixteen One Ton of Beer

chief pilot and my men that they were to stand down and await further instructions.

I was taken by the Captain in his jeep to a military encampment 3 miles away. There I entered the tent of the commanding general and stood in front of his desk. He continued to read and sign documents. A few minutes later while I cleared my throat a few times. He looked up at me and said, "What the hell do you want!"

I replied, "General, I have come a long way from Brazil in South America and am very hot and thirsty. The least you can do is offer me a can of cold beer."

He looked up at me and laughed, "You have a hell of a nerve to ask me for a cold beer!"

He went on to say, "I haven't seen a can of cold beer for months and I would also like one."

I replied, "General, that is an emergency. Where is the nearest cold beer?"

He said, "That would be at Kudna Air Force Base."

I asked, "How far is that from here?"

He replied, "About 120 miles."

I told him that if he would provide a senior military officer to accompany one of my helicopters, I would arrange for that helicopter to bring back to Enugnu a ton of beer. to be brought back from Kudna.

He said, "Do you mean that?

I said "Yes, Sir." He said, "I will go myself."

The General accompanied me back to the Engunu Air Field. I instructed the chief pilot to assign one of the helicopters to go to the Kudna Air Force Base. He would pick up a transport of one tone of cold beer and return to Engunu. The Brigadier General would travel as co-pilot.

I went back into Engunu and visited the Red Cross Encampment Radio Shack. I sent a message via Red Cross radio to the American Ambassador at Lagos

"Arrived at Enugnu at 12:30 today and affected my first delivery of one ton of relief supplies at 1300 hours."

The contents of that message were relayed to the State Department and White House.

Within hours New York and Washington newspapers carried the story of how speedy the United States response had met the difficulty in Nigeria. In the meantime, General Gowan canceled his persona non grata policy and the diplomatic situation returned to normal.

The Ambassador sent a message to me requesting clarification of the contents of the first relief mission. In a classified Top Secret response I advised him he did not have a need to know. He was very upset and asked me to return to Lagos within a month to receive his appreciation for the prompt way I handled the difficulty without going into details.

Truck convoys were arriving from Lagos weekly with needed supplies and returning the shipments of enbombed bodies to be repatriated to the United States. These were comprised mainly of nuns and priests recovered from the Biaferan war area who had been assonated.

I returned to Lagos a month and half later to attend a function at the American Embassy where I was to receive acknowledgment for my services in Nigeria. While there the Ambassador took me out of the room and whispered to me quietly what comprised the first ton of relief supplies that I had affected at Engunu. I again whispered quietly in his ear that he didn't have a need to know.

Chapter Sixteen One Ton of Beer

He said, "Mr. Hyder, I am the Ambassador. Do not talk down to me."

I took his arm and whispered quietly in his ear and said, "If you need to know, Mr. Ambassador, it was a ton of cold beer picked up from the Kaduna Air Force Base for the use of the Commanding General in Biafra."

He looked at me in consternation and said, "You used an American flag carrier to transport a ton of beer?"

I said, "Yes sir, Mr. Ambassador, it appeared to me to be the right thing to do at the time. This was to overcome the difficulties confronting the United States' mission to Nigeria. Mr. Ambassador, I had previously responded to you that you did not have a need to know."

He looked up at me and said quietly, "Please forget that I even asked."

I returned to Engunu and continued with my activities there. My relationships continued very satisfactorily without the Biafrian officials. All of my efforts were met with success.

Two months later I was reassigned to Lagos where a new staff position for me had been established. I returned to Brazil and brought my family to Lagos, Nigeria. My new supervisor would be Emmet Thomason. I also became Scout Master of B.S. troop at the American International School of Lagos. I further participated on staff of the Boy Scouts of Nigeria Wood Badge training program.

Our residence in Lagos was located on the water canal from Lagos to Benin. I purchased a cabin boat that I used for fishing and to take my family to the American beach west of Lagos. We went to the beach every weekend and enjoyed the opportunity with our friends. Sheila was pregnant at this time.

One weekend we were traveling downriver along the break water toward the American beach. On that trip I saw an unusually high wave of more than 8 feet approaching, and fearing that we might turn over, I told everyone to hang on. I gave the engine full power, faced into the wave, and my boat appeared to sit on the stern trying to climb the wave which finally passed under us. Sheila lost her balance and fell into the boat on her side which we learned had caused her to miscarry. The following week the doctor told us Sheila had lost the baby.

In November 1968 we traveled in our boat north up the coast in accompany with the Thomason's boat to Benin where we spent the weekend. We returned on Sunday to Lagos about 100 miles south.

In December 1968 we went home on leave to California and spent a great time with Sheila's parents.

In March 1969 we returned to Lagos and resumed our duties there.

In the spring of 1970 I ended my assignment in Nigeria and was transferred to Washington, D.C. After leaving Lagos on our way home we flew to Madrid, Spain. We rented a Volkswagen bug. We spent four days in Madrid visiting museums and art galleries and hen traveled from Madrid to Grenada and Barcelona, then along the southern coast of Spain, heading west. Our ten suitcases were tied to the rack on top of the Volkswagen. It appeared we were as high as we were long!

Chapter Sixteen One Ton of Beer

Chapter seventeen
The Phillipines

CHAPTER SEVENTEEN THE PHILLIPINES

We headed west along the coast stopping at various castles and tourist attractions. We followed the coast through Portugal to Lisbon. We visited many fantastic restaurants and enjoyed the fish delicacies at Istaliff. At Sharon's insistence we visited the famous Shrine of Fatima and after two nights returned to Lisbon. We then packed our bags and departed for Washington, D.C. via Pan Am. Sheila and family went to California to be with her parents while I met with officials of the State Department.

The Under Secretary of State for Africa, Dick Cashin, called me to his office and asked me if I would go to Rwanda, Burundi as the Chief of the Mission. This would have been a great promotion but when I asked Sheila's opinion, she said "No!" since she and the family could not accompany me to the new post; Dick Cashin was unhappy with my decision and I knew I had lost an opportunity to improve my professional career. I met the same day with the Director of the Mission to the Philippines to head a massive relief effort there due to damage from a major typhoon that devastated the area.

I agreed and left the next day for Manila. When I arrived there (July 1970), I reported to Joe Whelton, Division Chief of the Office of Community Development (C.D.) I went up to Los Banos and met the Governor, Felycisomo San Luis.

He and I became great friends and I had a room at the Pagsanjan Hotel which became my headquarters for the relief effort.

In meeting the hunger needs of all the displaced people, my colleague, Bert Fraleigh, originated the idea of a massive feed of a highly portable nutritious bread roll similar to a Parker House roll which was called a "Nutria-Bun." We prepared a simple recipe and provided 50 pound bags of flour to every Philippine baking facility which would produce the "Nutri-Buns."

The "Nutri-Buns" were packaged in sealed plastic bags, a dozen in a bag that could be air dropped from helicopters to people stranded by the rising flood waters. With this method, we were able to feed more than two million (2,000,000) people daily.

The big typhoon that hit the Philippines wiped out more than 10,000 homes. Most of these were in the poorest section of Metro Manila. More than 2,000,000 people had lost their homes.

I was placed in charge of setting up new homes and livelihood for the displaced survivors. I set up new communities beyond the boundary of Metro Manila. Some of these areas were Carmona, Sapang, Palay, and others.

Chapter Seventeen The Phillipines

The project involved building new homes, neighborhood schools, electric power, hospitals, portable water systems, and establishing a means of livelihood for each family. I went to nearby military disposal dumps and arranged for truck loads of material to be delivered to the new communities. These efforts were criticized by members of the United States Congress who wanted to see big ticket items like dams, electrification, and communication projects. I responded to the Congressional communities that my mandate was to reach the poorest of the poor and enable them to start new lives.

I was also assigned as a Public Administration Advisor to her Excellency Imelda Marcos, the Governor of Metro Manila, and had an office in her building.

To assist the resettled families I set up a program to provide each one with two female rabbits, two female piglets, and four chickens. I also sent one of my farm advisors to visit each family with a male rabbit and a male pig in order to procreate the families' animals. I also set up cottage industries to turn rabbit furs into gloves and clothing.

Sheila and the children arrived in December 1970. I became the Scout Master of the B.S. troop at the International School in Manila and became the Greater Manila Area Commissioner of Scouting. My old friend, Hank Byroade, arrived as the new Ambassador to the Philippines. It was good to have him in the driver's seat again. He promptly designated me as the Scouting Attaché of Embassy. His wife, Vidka, called me on the phone and asked me to come by their residence to talk to their two sons who had been members of my scout troop at Kabul,

Afghanistan. They were now teenagers and giving their mother some difficulty. I made arrangements for giving them more responsibility in the scouting program.

In the spring of 1971, I arranged for the first of many camporees to be held on the Island of Corregidor. At my first encampment there we had 50 B.S.A. scouts and more than 100 scouts from the Boy Scouts of the Philippines (B.S.P.)

This was a 3-day encampment. Towards the end of the second day I became alarmed along with my staff when scouts returned to camp carrying live grenades, guns, bayonets, and miscellaneous armament left over from World War II. I instructed my staff to collect all unexploded munitions and take to a designated area safely away from the encampment.

After our final campfire we returned to Manila and I contacted the Philippine Army Corp of Engineers. I requested that they be sent to Corregidor to clean up the island and arrange safe disposal of all military debris found there, in particular live ammunitions.

In the summer of 1972 we had our second encampment on Corregidor. The Girl Scouts of the Philippines (G.S.P.) were invited to attend. The participants now exceeded 300 scouts.

At my staff meeting on the second day of encampment, a B.S.A. Scout Master told me that they had hiked to the top of the mountain where the World War II Military Cemetery was located. There was a flag pole mounted there which had faded pieces of square cloth. We were told that it was supposed to be an American flag but we could not identify it as such. I asked the assembled adults what did they recommend be done; they said they would take one of the American flags being used by one of the attending troops and have it raised over the World War II cemetery, to honor the American veterans buried there.

When we returned to Manila I contacted the Chairman of the Philippine Wartime Cemetery and Monuments Commission. They were responsible for maintaining the cemeteries and providing flags as required.

They told me their budget was not sufficient to carry out their responsibility. I further told him that as long as American scouting remained in the Philippines, the B.S.A. would replace any damaged American flags with new flags upon receipt of the damaged one.

The greater Manila area scouting program represented five B.S.A. troops, 2 Cub Scout units, and an Explorer Sea Scout unit. In the overall Philippine District there were also two additional units, Girl Scout unit, and Cub Scout troops at Clark United States Air Force Base and Subic Naval Base. The District Chairman of the Philippine scouting district, the Far East Council headed by the Clark Air Force Base, 7th Air Force Commanding Officer, Major General Leroy Manors. The Philippine District also had a professionally paid B.S.A. executive. The greater Manila area contained the largest American commercial activity in the district; I was relied upon to obtain contributions through the American Chamber of Commerce and other American commercial establishments to support the professional B.S.A. executive for the Philippine District. My scouting umbrella also included the Girl Scouts of America headed by Ann Butler, an L.D.S. volunteer leader. As the greater Manila scouting commissioner and chairman, I coordinated all area scouting activities. I arranged for a contest by the scouts to come up with a single name and symbol to represent their area. The American Chamber of Commerce and other scouting supporting entities welcomed the single scout contribution request.

In 1972 my son Mark completed and received his Eagle Rank at a B.S.A. National Court of Honor and participated in most of my activities as the Senior Patrol

Leader (S.P.L.). My son Craig also received his Life Rank at that National Court of Honor. I also received the District Award of Merit called "The Order of the Golden Carabao" for distinguished service in promoting programs for scouts.

In 1973 we were all known as the Greater Manila Area Scouts, and wore printed tee shirts and neckerchiefs. Our new symbol was adopted and was two entwined circles, one with the B.S.A. emblem and one with the G.S.A. emblem. This new symbol was printed on all of our new tee shirts and worn by all scouts and leaders of the greater Manila area. Management of scouting in the Philippines proceeded without any difficulties and our programs met with success.

In June 1973 I was asked to attend a Far East Council B.S.A. National Court of Honor in Seoul, Korea. Sheila and I went there by commercial air. I was honored to receive the top council recognition called the "Silver Beaver." This was given to me by Major General Joe Stillwell.

In the fall of 1973 we received an official visit from the National President of the B.S.A. We honored him with a dinner at the American Embassy Club official where we presented him with one of our new tee shirts. He was very pleased to receive it and said he would show it off when he returned to the United States. It is my understanding that he did so. When he appeared at a National meeting of scouting wearing the new symbol of the Greater Manila Area Scouting, the National representative of the G.S.A. took exception for our use of the G.S.A. emblem thereof. This had been done without the G.S.A. permission and said that the B.S.A. would be sued accordingly. As a result thereof, it was my understanding that the President of the B.S.A. resigned.

Scouting in the Philippines continued with the current arrangement without any difficulties from either youth association.

In early 1974 I received an invitation from the President Manual Syquis of the B.S.P. to attend a Philippine B.S. National Court of Honor at Davao in Mindanao scheduled for 18 May 1974 where I received the B.S.P. gold medal for outstanding services provided to the B.S.P. I was also to learn that Major General Manor had also received an invitation and would be attending. He would receive the top B.S.P. recognition at that Court of Honor. He told me that he and his wife would be flying to Davao and Sheila and I were invited to accompany in his plane.

My friend, Bill Quasha, was a member of the Executive Board of the B.S.P and was a staff member of the National Court of Honor. He was a prominent attorney in Manila and had been General MacArthur's legal advisor. In the picture depicting General MacArthur's legal advisor landing on Luzon, Philippines ("I have returned!"), Bill Quasha walked 10 feet behind General MacArthur when they came ashore in Luzon, Philippines.

Bill was to become my co-leader in the greater Manila boy scouting program. He was also to become my co-director of the upcoming historical camporee on Corregidor and the reenactment of the infamous Bataan Death March.

In early 1974 we went home leave and stopped at Taipei, Taiwan. Sheila and I visited a well-known sailing

Chapter seventeen The Phillipines

ship builder and signed a contract for construction of a 43-foot sailing yacht.

We then continued to fly to the United States stopping at Oahu, Hawaii for a week's vacation of rest and relaxation.

We enjoyed our home leave at Mi-Wuk Village, California, which is in Tuolumne County at an elevation of 5,000 feet.

We returned to Manila in October, 1974. At the end of November we took delivery of our beautiful new sailing yacht and joined the Manila Yacht Club. This became the new home of our yacht, the "Mi-No-Wuk. II." People would ask me what the name meant; I said, "Me No Work." I also hired a Philippine boat boy and his wife who lived aboard in the forward crew cabin of the Mi-No-Wuk II. They kept our yacht in "Bristol" condition.

I had a telescope in my office in the Embassy building on the 4th floor which enabled me to see my yacht and would from time-to-time call my boat boy and give him instructions to prepare for my arrival at lunch and would go aboard with guests from the Embassy and power out through the harbor for a long lunch.

The power plant on my vessel was a 75-Volvo Penta diesel engine which gave us adequate power when not under sail. I also ordered a second set of sails including a large Genoa and a storm staysail and a Drifter sail.

We often participated in yacht club races in Manila bay and the South China Sea. My foredeck mate was a blue-eyed Cuban National who had escaped from Cuba and was an asset aboard.

To effectively race my vessel a crew of 10 to 12 were required to handle all sails that sometimes numbered 5 to 7 sails. We raced the boat from Manila to Hong Kong through the South China Sea and made one round trip race to Singapore.

We were delighted with my new acquisition. Sheila and I used our master cabin which was mid-ship. Sheila would not come aboard the long China Sea races since she was not happy with my first mate's colorful language.

Twelve (12) boys and girls, 14 to 18 years of age, approached me and asked me to form a Sea Scout unit. They were all interested in small boat ailing and boat handling and to me was a de'ja-vu when I was 14 and 15 years old. This resulted in our forming a co-ed Sea Scout ship. The unit was registered as part of the Philippine Far East Council and I became their skipper and my wife, Sheila, became one of the mates since it was a co-ed unit requiring a female leader. I enjoyed their participation as the crew of the Min-No-Wuk II. We made another number of sailing trips to Corregidor, Mariveles, Bataan, and also Subic Naval Base.

As a consequence thereto our district President General Manors appointed me as the Sea Scout Commodore of those units.

One of our sailing outings was to Subic Naval Base and a few days later we were on our return to Manila. Our Sea Scout vessel under sail had entered Manila Bay and was heading south for the Manila Yacht Club five miles distant when three Philippine naval vessels were approaching from the stern. The leading vessel gave three blasts on their horn to get us to divert from their line of approach. I instructed my helmsman to hold steady on course and to another crew member to hoist my Commodore flag.

CHAPTER SEVENTEEN THE PHILLIPINES

Since we were under sail and the Philippine vessel is under power my vessel had the right of way. The Philippine vessels promptly changed course and proceeded around us.

A week later I had occasion to visit the Philippine Navy Headquarters to discuss our upcoming camporee on Corregidor. The Senior Philippine Naval Officer asked me who was the Commodore at the American Embassy.

I replied, "I was" and he said, "I wondered because I was on the destroyer that was diverted by a sail boat ahead of us."

During my work at the Embassy I met with a Philippine Brigadier General who was in command of the Philippine Green Berets. I had told the General that I was arranging for a special five day hike to the north of the Island of Luzon. He asked me if I thought my scouts were up to this type of activity since they would have to cross two rivers carrying their packs. I told him not to underestimate our young souls, that they were more capable than people expected. He told me he would render any assistance that we would require.

The Ambassador called me the next day for a meeting and asked me if I had taken into consideration that our routing would take us into some disputed territory of Philippine dissidents.

I replied that I had already met with the military Commandant of the area concerned and he had assured me that there would be no difficulty. Both B.S.A/B.S.P. and G.S.A/ G.S.P. scouts would make up the group on this scouting event.

I was called in by the head of the Girl Scouts of the Philippines who questioned me about the safety of her girls in a co-ed encampment. I assured her that all would go well in my experience with co-ed activities and had never encountered any difficulties. She appeared unconvinced and said she would go along with it and hope for the best.

My son Mark was the Senior Patrol leader of this expedition and led the way. The hike from our departure point to the campout location was approximately 15 miles. The scouts handled each difficulty in their stride and arrived safely at the campout location and set up their tents in the areas designated.

It took 7 to 10 hours for the group to reach the encampment. Some of the leaders and scouts noticed Philippine military along their rout of march approximately three-fourths to one mile away from the hike route. This was in keeping with what the General had said that the safety of my young people would be paramount and assured.

When the next morning arrived I was confronted by two of the Girl Scout leaders representing the G.S.P. and the G.S.A. who said they were disappointed to learn from their girls that the boy scouts had raided their encampment removing intimate underwear from the clothesline.

I was very concerned and called a meeting of all my scout leaders to discuss these charges. I told them to investigate and return to me in one hour to discuss their findings. This they did. Reporting after talking to all of the Boy Scout leaders they could find no evidence that the boys had participated in any raids on the Girl Scout camp. Two hours later the Girl Scout leaders arrived with two of the senior Girl Scouts who apologized to me and reported that the Girl Scouts had fabricated their story

Chapter seventeen The Phillipines

due to a lack of attention from the boys.

On the night of the final campfire after all the songs and activities were completed, everyone stood and performed our closing song and prayers. As we stood to depart we were surprised when colorful lights appeared out of the darkness around the camping area and the military brigade band marched in and started to play contemporary dance music. The boys and girls sat down in their areas when the General gave a brief talk complimenting all of the young people on their performance during this campout.

He then said, "Let's close the encampment with fun.

The band will now play and you are all encouraged to join in the dancing." The girls looked over at the boys and the boys looked over at the girls; suddenly the Philippine Boy Scouts went over to the American Girl Scouts and asked them to dance.

The American boys, not to be outdone, soon followed. A great time was had by all and the next day we returned to Manila.

A few days later I received a call from the leader of the G.S.P. She apologized to me for her concern and said she had earned a new respect for the way all of the scouts had performed.

During the 1974 camporee on Corregidor, my staff noted the dilapidated condition of the flag pole located at top sides of Corregidor. We contacted the United States Army Corps of Engineers in the Philippines, who agreed to lift the old flag pole from Corregidor and transport it to Subic Naval Base. There they would repair it and reinstall it at Corregidor. Historically speaking this was the flag pole that General MacArthur spoke about when he re-conquered the Island of Corregidor from the Japanese.

He had stood before it and said, "I see the old flag pole still stands; raise our colors and let no other enemy of Freedom ever haul it down again."

In early 1975 the old flag pole, completely refurbished and painted white, was carried by a heavy duty helicopter from Subic to Corregidor to its original site on "Top Side." Our arrangements for the Far East Council camporee on Corregidor went forward as planned.

Invitations were sent to all scouting associations in the Western Pacific Rim: i.e. Japan, Okinawa, Australia, New Zealand, Taiwan, South Vietnam, all Embassies in the Philippines and B.S.P/G.S.P. Provinces. We received acknowledgments and intent to participate from more than 3,500 scouts and leaders.

The location of the proposed encampment would be on Corregidor and we would have scout representation from all countries that were involved in World War II.

The United States Air Force agreed to provide and staff of a 200-bed field hospital on a designated location on the Island of Corregidor to meet any medical needs. The geographic layout included four separate camps with representative headquarter staff for each camp. Camp Four was to be all Girl Scouts and leaders. The Philippine Army Corps of Engineers agreed to provide communication installation between each camp and headquarters.

They also agreed to provide and install portable water resources at each encampment. The logistics in providing food and swimming safely had also been met.

Everything appeared to be proceeding on schedule.

We had arranged with the Philippine Navy to provide

landing ship transportation (LST) from Manila to Corregidor. A week before the scheduled encampment we were notified that a major typhoon was approaching the Philippines. I received some recommendations to cancel the activity. After consultation with weather specialists and reviewing the anticipated path of the storm I appeared on television and announced that the camporee would proceed as planned. I was advised that the weather front would move northeast away from the Philippines after passing Guam.

Invitations were also sent to President Ferdinand Marcos and Governor Imelda Marcos to attend the camporee. Invitations were also sent to the American Ambassador as well as all Ambassadors in the Philippines.

The historical camporee was a great success. More than 150 of the scouts signed up to participate in the re-enactment of the infamous Bataan Death March which was to take place following the closure of the camporee.

"BATAAN DEATH MARCH"

The logistic planning required that we provide for a medical support team, food detail, a passenger bus, and ambulance to accompany the marchers. Bill Quaska and I were co-hike directors; my son Mark was one of the senior patrol leaders. The marchers walked for approximately 80 miles along the original route of march in temperatures to 90 to 104 degrees. All backpacks of the marchers were carried to tru0cks to each encampment in advance of the arrival of the marchers. The destination of the death march was the original Japanese Prison Camp (Camp O'Donnell.)

We would be stopping at various villages along the original route of the march to our ultimate destination.

During the original Death March there were approximately 20,000 Americans and more than 50,000 Philippino marchers. Whenever an allied captive, many of whom had sustained battle wounds faltered or fell down, a Japanese soldier would bayonet the prisoner and kick the body to the side of the road leaving it there.

Occasionally when passing a village sometimes a member of that village would offer a sip of water or a bite of food try to help the passing prisoners. Many times these Philippine "angels of mercy" in their attempts to help, and were shot or bayoneted by the Japanese guards. We presented the head of each village with a plaque acknowledging their heroic efforts members of their villages who risked their lives to try to help the marchers.

On the 5th day of the march we reached Mt. Samat.

We rested overnight and had a campfire and listened to survivors of the original Death March talk about their experiences and those of lost comrades during that march. We continued up the trail in the days that followed and when necessary put some of the marchers on the bus for rest. The official records indicate that more than 20% of the original marchers died on that infamous march at the hands of the ruthless Japanese guards.

The Associated Press accompanied our march and had a photographer record the event. It was released and aired on television in 1979 in the United States. The horrors that occurred to the participants of the original Death March were considered to be one of the worst atrocities that occurred during World War II.

Chapter seventeen The Phillipines

The march stopped for lunch on each day and was given peanut butter and jelly sandwiches and Kool Aid which were prepared by a team of adults headed by Janet Baker, Sheila Hyder, Ann Butler, and other scout leaders.

The food and drink were considered to be power sustenance given to help sustain the participants during this difficult march. There were a few that took advantage of the accompanying bus when they felt too weak to continue. It is a tribute to the fighting spirit of these young people who took the time and effort and continued after the march to complete required distance. Certificates were presented to all successful participants of the march, signed by Bill Quasha and myself who were very proud of their perseverance and achievement. The Bataan Death March became a recognized B.S.A./G.S.A. authorized activity recognized and achievement for a historical trail award.

CHAPTER SEVENTEEN THE PHILLIPINES

Chapter Eightteen
The Viet Nam Evacuation

Chapter Eightteen The Viet Nam Evacuation

In 1975 the United States terminated its offensive in Vietnam and withdrew all our troops. Philip Habib, the Deputy United States Ambassador to Vietnam, was appointed to head up a United States commission to meet with officials of North Vietnam at Hanoi. They would negotiate the termination of hostilities and the end of the Vietnamese War.

I was designated by the American Ambassador in Manila as a special consul to process evacuees from Vietnam for onward movement to the United States. A platoon of Marines was assigned to me at Clark Air Force Base to assist in this purpose. As soon as the United States had decided to evacuate Vietnam, notice was sent throughout the country notifying everyone who had supported the American cause by fraternization, etc., to leave immediately using all resources available. There was a major exodus of all contract personnel, employees of the United States Military Assistant Command, Vietnam (MAC-V), American Embassy (Amer/Emb), U.S. Information Service (USIA), and U.S. Agency for International Development (USAID). All these persons were to leave Vietnam immediately prior to the arrival of the Viet Kong taking over the rest of South Vietnam. There was a continuous air lift from Saigon to Clark Air Force Base in the Philippines. The United States Navy provided transportation and protection with a miscellaneous fleet of ships that carried thousands of evacuees from Vietnam to the Philippines.

All of these evacuees were transported overland by bus to my processing center at Clark Air Force Base.

A number of incidents took place during this process. One such incident was the arrival of the President of South Vietnam, Nguyen-Cao-Ky. When he appeared before me I stood up and welcomed him but noticed he was still carrying side arms.

I signaled to the Marine Sergeant and called him and instructed him to disarm the General. They took his weapons and grenades they found in his pocket. He objected and said, "I am the President of Vietnam and am entitled to protect myself." I told him he was now in the territory of the United States and he would be treated like every other American. I was also confronted by military sergeants and non-commissioned officers (NCOs) who introduced accompanying women as their wives and sisters. Upon careful review, I directed all uniformed military personnel to be reunited with their units. All undocumented women and children were sent to the Island of Guam for further processing. I gave military personnel who claimed that some of the women were attached to them, an instruction sheet of how those women could be located upon arrival in the United States. Most of the women who arrived at my processing center had previously been working in bars in Saigon and had to be medically examined prior to onward movement to camps in the United States.

Chapter Eightteen The Viet Nam Evacuation

There were many other men and women who arrived at my processing center who had been employees of the American Embassy and the United States Military Command, Vietnam. They were also sent to Guam and were medically cleared and issued green cards for entering into the United States. Among this latter group I was very pleased to find my two Vietnamese secretaries who had worked in my office in Saigon and had safely arrived.

One of the major difficulties facing the evacuation from Vietnam was the status of the Vietnamese mothers, and their infant's father by American military. We had been advised that the Viet Kong and North Vietnamese would order the death of mothers and children identified as such. The World Council of Churches (W.C.C,) had requested that a special "Baby List" be arranged for these babies and mothers out of Vietnam identified as children of American military forces.

We arranged for a large American Air Force aircraft to transport them to my processing center at Clark Air Force Base. It was also arranged for American female volunteers to assist in caring for those children when they arrived at my station. Many of these women were dependents of United States military and American civilians in Vietnam who assisted the W.C.C. My wife, Sheila, was among the women volunteers. The "Baby Lift" aircraft was capable of carrying more than 300 children.

I was in continuous contact with the pilot of that aircraft and was notified when he started its takeoff roll from Saigon, and was horrified a moment later, to learn they were under fire by Viet Kong. The plane ended up in a rice patty at the end of the runway. Only a few babies and volunteers were injured and a second flight took off successfully and landed at Clark Air Force Base. I became involved in a difficulty when my wife told me that she had fallen in love with a particular female infant and wanted to adopt the infant. I told her I could not make an exception for her as I had received similar request from other female volunteers and that all children would have to proceed to a processing center in the United States and would be placed in approved homes in accordance with approved procedures. My wife became very depressed and it was many months before she overcame her displeasure with me.

CORBIS/Bettmann
Evacuees are helped aboard an Air America helicopter perched atop a Saigon building on April 29, 1975. The evacuation site was one of many from which Americans and foreign nationals were evacuated to waiting Navy ships.

Photography courtesy of Corbis Image Library

CHAPTER EIGHTTEEN THE VIET NAM EVACUATION

Chapter Nineteen
The Hospital

Chapter Nineteen The Hospital

In November 1975 I received a call from the American Ambassador who asked me to come to his office in Manila. He had received a classified message involving me.

He asked me, "What was the date you received your Eagle Rank in the boy Scouts?"

I asked, "Why is this coming up after all these years?"

He told me that I had been nominated for a very prestigious recognition. I was more confused than ever.

I asked him what it was about.

He said, "You have been nominated at the highest level to receive a special award called the distinguished <u>Eagle Scout Award</u>."

I knew was a very special recognition ad a prestigious award for which I would have been very proud to have received.

A few weeks earlier I had heard a rumor from someone that my friend Bill Quasha, holder of the highest recognition in scouting had mentioned me in a letter sent to the National Office of the B.S.A. I had heard nothing further.

I had completed all requirements for Eagle Rank in 1939, and was scheduled to receive it at the next National Court of Honor which had been scheduled for November of that year.

My life had been overtaken by events when I received activation orders from President Roosevelt requiring me to report for active duty within 24 hours to the Commandant, First Naval District, Boston, Massachusetts on 15 October 1939.

As a consequence I had never *formally* received my Eagle Rank.

Maurice receiving the Eagle Scout Award

Distinguished Eagle Scout Award

Chapter Nineteen The Hospital

Chapter Twenty
Mi No Wuk II

Chapter Twenty Mi No Wuk II

I n mid-1977 I was in contact with my backstop officer at the State Department, Washington, D.C. I had previously requested that I be separated and retired from the State Department at my post, the American Embassy, Manila, Philippines. At that time they concurred and said that I would have to have my separation physical completed at the Clark Air Force Base hospital prior to retirement. In that physical it was recommended that I have a left hernia repair prior to retirement. I agreed to comply with those orders.

The purpose of requesting separation at Manila was to be able to sail my yacht, the 43-fiit seagoing "Mi-No-Wuk II" from the Philippines to the west coast of the United States of America.

I had been preparing my yacht for that purpose and had acquired three heavy duty 12 volt, 20-AMP batteries. I had installed two banks of solar charges on the mizzen mast at the juncture of the mizzen gaff. This arrangement would provide adequate electricity of 110 volts for my refrigerator and freezer installed in the galley plus all navigation and radio electronics aboard. I had also loaded 50 miscellaneous beverages, i.e., San Miguel beer, Scotch, and bourbon as ballast. I had anticipated that the voyage from Manila west through the Indian Ocean north through the Red Sea, and Suez Canal, and west through the Mediterranean, and across the Atlantic to the United States would take a minimum of one year. Ultimately I would go through the Panama Canal into the Pacific and north to San Diego, California. A number of volunteers offered to be members of my crew for this sailing endeavor. Sheila did not want to be aboard for the entire trip and said she would fly to various ports in advance of our arrival. She would be in communication with me by radio each day.

I had been receiving letters from some of my Manila Yacht Club friends who had preceded me sailing to the United States along the same proposed routing. They reported to me of some of the incidents they had encountered off the Island of Ceylon when they went north through the Red Sea heading toward the Suez Canal where they had encountered trouble from pirates off the Horn of Africa. According to my military contacts I had acquired a bazooka along with 36 rounds of ammunition and a Browning automatic rifle (BAR), also with ammunition. I was preparing my yacht for the planned trip west. I also loaded 12 cases of canned food for emergency rations aboard, along with 12 cases of water.

In the first week of September 1977 I went to the

Chapter Twenty Mi No Wuk ii

hospital at Clark Air Force Base to receive the hernia repair surgery. This was required by the State Department prior to my retirement.

I was assigned to a flag officer's hospital room for my recovery. I told Sheila that everything went very well in the surgery and that I thought I would be released in a couple of days. Fifteen (15) minutes later I reached out and grabbed Sheila's hand and said, "I'm in pain; it hurts like hell!

Sheila went out into the hallway and yelled to the nurse, "Mr. Hyder's having a heart attack!"

The nurses arrived quickly and told me the cardiologist was on his way. Shortly thereafter the cardiologist and six interns rushed into the room.

The cardiologist listened to my heart with his stethoscope stepped back and asked his interns quickly, "Tell me what's wrong with Mr. Hyder." Four of the interns claimed I was having a heart attack; the other two claimed they weren't sure.

The cardiologist turned to the interns and said, "Mr. Hyder's not having a heart attack! He has paricarditis. You should know the difference."

I looked up at the doctor and said, "Doc, I'm in pain, help me."

He promptly injected me with a needle in my chest and told me he was giving me morphine which quickly relieved me from the pain. He told me I was going to have to spend a few more days in the hospital until I recovered from the paricarditis. Someone had notified the State Department of this new turn of events.

I received a new decision from the State Department

which posed a new dilemma for me.

The State Department decision now required me to return to Washington, D.C. for separation and retirement. My plans to sail my yacht back to the United States was in jeopardy. That afternoon General Manors paid me a visit; he asked me how I was doing and asked if there was anything he could do to be of further assistance. I told him about the decision made by the State Department and the dilemma now facing me.

He said, "Let's get Admiral Tom Kilcline in on this."

He then picked up the phone in my recovery room and called Tom; he told him about my current difficulty reminding him that my vessel was berthed at Subic Naval Base asking for his recommendation.

He replied, "Tell Maury Hyder not to worry and that he would send one of his senior officers to me at Clark with documents to sign and they will take care of the rest."

A Navy Commander arrived the next day, produced the necessary papers, and showed me where to sign.

He said, "All arrangements have been made to transport the "Mi-No-Wuk II" to the west coast."

I asked him, "What would my responsibility be and what do I need to do?"

He said, "You will have to arrange for construction of a cradle to hold your 35-ton yacht and that a heavy duty barge with a 50-ton crane had to be contracted for at your expense."

I asked him, "When would this take place?"

He said, "You will be advised."

Sheila and I returned to Manila on the 15th of September. Two weeks later I was to learn that Major General Manors

Chapter Twenty Mi No Wuk II

was going to receive his 3rd Star making him a Lieutenant General. I extended an invitation to General Manors and his lady to be guests at Manila on 15 November 1977. He and his lady arrived at Manila a week later and were our guests of honor at the American Embassy Club on Rojas Boulevard. As part of our congratulations we presented him with his 2-1/2 star promotion. It should be noted that General Manor could not receive his 3rd star until both his feet were on the plane to Pearl Harbor. I was later to learn that his new assignment would be as Deputy Commander-in-Chief, Pacific, and would be assigned to Pearl Harbor.

I received my home leave and separation orders from the State Department on 5 December 1977. We were packed up lock, stock, and barrel, and departed by 15 December. I went to Washington, D.C. while Sheila and the children went to our home leave address at Mi-Wuk Village, California.

A nessage was received dated 10 December from Admiral Kilcline stating that the "Mi-No-Wuk II" had been approved for shipment to the United States. It would be carried aboard a United States aircraft carrier and be off-loaded at the United States Naval Base at San Diego, California in early January 1978. I would be notified by the Navy Department accordingly.

I notified my cousin, Bill Ferris, who was a United States Navy Commandeer for his assistance in helping me receive my sailing yacht in San Diego. His duty station was at the United States Navy Base, San Diego. I told him that when I was notified about the expected date of arrival of the "Min-No-Wuk II" that Craig and I would arrive in San Diego to take delivery. It should be noted that when

The Mi No Wuk II

Chapter Twenty Mi No Wuk II

the Subic Naval Base was issuing hull numbers of private boats then located at the base, my vessel received the identifying number NV-001.

Craig and I went to San Diego 9 January 1978 and met with Commander Bill Ferris and watched the aircraft carrier entering its mooring at the San Diego Naval Base. It was good to see the "Mi-No-Wuk II" strapped to the top deck of the aircraft carrier. As soon as the ship was tied to the pier and the brow was in place, we went aboard. We asked to meet the skipper and were taken by the Marine guard up to his cabin. He said he was glad to meet the owner of the boat that he admired so much looking down at it from the bridge. He told me he would like to see what it looked like inside. I told him it would be my pleasure and reminded him I still had to clear customs in compliance with regulations on brining the yacht into the United States. He told me that he had already arranged for full customs clearance for my yacht when he stopped at Pearl Harbor and that all formalities had been met. I was appalled since I had considerable beverages loaded into the bottom as ballast. He said no further action on my part was required. I told him in order for him to go aboard I had to get the two masts removed from the top of the yacht and set on the deck so that we could go below. He had the ship's Chief Boson Mate arrange to remove the mast and set them on the deck so we could gain access into the cabin. He was amazed at the beauty of the layout of the cabins and the intricate carving of the cabinet ware, shelving, etc. He said he hoped he'd be able to see the boat after it would be in the water. I told him that I would invite him and his lady at his earliest convenience since the yacht would remain in the harbor of San Diego. He said he had to get down on the pier because his wife would be arriving momentarily. I lifted up one of the bottom floor boards and handed him 3 bottles of Scotch, Johnny Walker Black, Red, and Chives Regal, and told him please have a drink on the success of my vessel arriving at the Port of San Diego.

As we left the yacht I mentioned to him that I had asked permission from his Executive Officer for enough time to get a coat of bottom paint on the bottom of the hull prior to placing the yacht in the water, but that he had refused. He laughed and told me not to worry and he would take care of the Executive Officer and prepare the hull of the yacht as required. The yacht weighed 35-dead weight tons, and required the heavy lift to set it in the water, lifting and lowering the mast into position. The Chief Boson's Mate volunteered to arrange for the services of some sailors to assist in the cleaning the bottom and applying the copper based pain. He also said he would have a diesel mechanic check out my power plant once my yacht was in the water. Cleaning and painting the bottom was completed that afternoon and arrangements were made for heavy lift barge to come along side the next morning and lift the yacht into the water. The next morning at 10:00 a.m. the "Mi-No-Wuk II" was lifted off the top deck of the aircraft carrier and set into the water.

Bill had looked over the cradle and said it was all solid teak wood timbers and he wanted it. He would have it removed the next day to his furniture repair shop. I placed 2 fifty cent ($0.50) pieces, one at the main mast step and one at the mizzen mast step. This is an old sea-going

Chapter Twenty Mi No Wuk II

tradition for placing coins under the masts. With the help of Craig and some volunteer sailors we hooked up the various stays to secure both masts to the hull.

As previously arranged with the Boson's Mate, a diesel mechanic came aboard, checked the engine making sure that all was ready. We got it started and it purred beautifully. We gave our thanks to the Executive Officer and gave some monetary appreciation to those sailors who helped us.

With Commander Ferris and Craig aboard we got underway and moved north to the mooring buoys off of Harbor Drive.

We busied ourselves and made the "Mi-No-Wuk II" shipshape. We left Craig to stay on the yacht for security and I left with Bill to his home for the evening.

The next day at 11:00 a.m. Bill's wife Lillian, drove us to Harbor Drive, the location of the "Mi-No-Wuk II". With all aboard we headed for the submarine base at Point Loma to berth the yacht. As we approached the pier two Marines ran down and waived us away and said we could not tie up to that pier. Bill was in his uniform and told them that the Commanding Officer of the submarine base had given permission for the "Mi-No-Wuk II" to be tied up to that pier pending further instructions. The duty officer at the submarine base had come down to look at the yacht alongside his pier and had noted the numerical designation of NV-001.

He asked for my identification and military rank. I showed him my identification and told him that the Admiral at Subic Naval Base had assigned that number to conform to my American Embassy status.

He said he would notify his Commanding Officer and my yacht may have to be moved.

The next day Commander Ferris checked in with the Commanding Officer at the San Diego Naval Training Station and was told that due to the classified nature of the submarine base that we should move the "Mi-No-Wuk II" to the Naval Training Station pier. He further advised that he had been allocated a space for a personal boat on the pier and have never utilized it since he had no boat.

We moved the yacht from the submarine base to the Naval Training Station pier which became its permanent location in San Diego. We spent a week installing the various sails, rigging, and adjusting them as necessary. The next weekend Bill, Lillian, Sheila, Craig, and I took the yacht out into the Pacific on a day sail and picnic checking all of the standing and running rigging. Everything functioned well and up to our expectations.

It seemed that everyone at the Naval Station had made it their business to come down to inspect the new yacht on the pier. During the following months Sheila and I cruised south To Tijuana and Cabo San Lucas with various guests aboard. Our vessel had the capacity to sleep 12 people. We especially enjoyed crossing the Sea of Cortez and visiting Matzilan, then south to Acapulco where Sheila had friends who lived there.

In 1979 we sailed up the coast to San Francisco and enjoyed having many guests aboard. We arranged for the "Mi-No-Wuk II" to be moored at the St. Francis Yacht Club for three months. In 1980 we sailed back to San Diego and moored again at the Naval Training Station pier. Bill Ferris became custodian of the "Mi-

Chapter Twenty Mi No Wuk II

No-Wuk II" while Sheila and I returned to Mi-Wuk.

One day Bill approached me and said the Admiral of the Naval Training Station had asked to use the yacht and requested my permission to do so. I replied that I would be pleased to give that permission but needed to know: was he a sailor, or a sailor sailor?

He asked, "Explain what you mean?"

I said I knew he was a sailor but I was a sailor of the cloth.

He asked, "What do you mean?" I told him that while I had a diesel power plant aboard I used cloth sails for propulsion, and wanted to know if he had sailing boat experience. He said he thought he could handle it and what did he have to do. I suggested he come down the following weekend and sail the yacht around the Coronado Island. I would sit in the stern and observe. This he did.

He came aboard with two sailors and asked, "What next?"

I said, "You're the skipper. I'm going to sit back here and observe. Go ahead and take her out."

He took over the wheel, gave the necessary orders to raise the sails, and did a very credible job handling the yacht. We headed west out the harbor into the Pacific where he brought the yacht about and made both a starboard and port cast. Then we went out around the island. After three hours of sailing we returned to San Diego and he brought it up to the berth and secured the yacht. I told him "You're fully qualified and you can take the yacht out whenever it was free for use."

Bill would be the custodian as long as it was berthed in San Diego. Sheila discussed with me the long commute from Mi-Wuk to San Diego whenever we wanted to use the "Mi-No-Wuk II." Accordingly, we made arrangements to put the "Mi-No-Wuk II" on the market.

In 1978 we bought a Ford pickup to pull a boat and trailer so I could fish the nearby lakes. I also purchased a cab-over insert camper that provided us with more comfort on the road and at camp sites.

In June 1980 I received an offer from a United States Naval Commander, retired, who wanted to purchase the "Mi-No-Wuk II." He told me his children were all away at college; he and his wife wanted a boat like mine to make a trip around the world. He stated his house was up for sale and anticipated he would have the funds in ninety (90) days to complete the transaction. With great regret I complied and my dream with the "Mi-No-Wuk II" came to an end. During the next two months Bill and I would see the "Mi-No-Wuk II" at the local yacht club. In July 1981 Sheila and I went to the Cow Palace in San Francisco where all of the new boat models were on display. I was interested in a boat that would allow me to go offshore fishing and provide Sheila with a comfortable stateroom aboard.

We settled on a 26-foot cabin cruiser called a Barnegat with deep water capability. It came with a 330 horsepower (HP) Mer-cruiser power plant. It was provided with inboard bait wells and fish boxes. It was also capable of being placed on a trailer and towed behind a one ton truck. This boat was now known as the "Mi-No-Wuk III." It had the capability of sleeping four people comfortably.

Chapter Twenty Mi No Wuk II

Chapter Twenty One
The Boy Scouts of America

Chapter Twenty one The Boy Scouts of America

I'd arranged for a parking area on our property at Mi-Wuk Village for the boat with an overhead shed named "Snug Harbor." During the next five years we would use the "Mi-No-Wuk III" extensively. We launched our boat at Berkeley and visited many of the ports south of San Francisco such as Pacifica, Half Moon Bay, Santa Cruz, and Monterey. We would also launch our boat at Antioch and fish at San Pablo Bay and the Sacramento River for sturgeon and salmon. We would often spend more than four days on the river and berth at Stockton and along the inland waterway. We also took the boat up to Mt. Lassen and fished the lovely Eagle Lake for its fabulous trout.

We also spent many weekends at the nearby New Malones Lake and Beardsley Lake. One time we had our greatest big trout fishing with my son Mark, nephew Paul, and fishing buddy, Mike Blackstone, aboard when we limited out with trophy sized trout.

Following my retirement to Tuolumne County, I became the Counsel Commissioner of the Yosemite Area B.S.A. I had become very proficient in teaching survival in the Sierra Nevada Mountains. I arranged for a survival trek over the Sierra for a group of Senior Scouts, 14-18 years of age, along with three adult leaders and myself. All participants would carry their own packs and includes therein only one days' ration of food.

All further meals were to come from the vegetation and the lakes and streams around us which provided us with fish. We built snares for small rodents and captured snakes when available.

The scouts who hesitated initially at this new diet soon came to like their food and found the barbequed snake chunks as a delicacy. Our trek took us up to 11,000 feet starting from the top of Sonora Pass, up to the John Muir Trail, then down the mountains and came out at Bell Meadow. We ate tuber roots which we collected from swampy areas which looked and tasted like potatoes.

We also identified wild onions, wild garlic, watercress, and miner's lettuce.

The entire trek covered approximately 15 miles. We came out at Bell Meadow where the scout's parents and Sheila awaited us. One of the adults in our group carried a forestry radio and maintained communication with our parental group when we would arrive at Bell Meadow.

At our last campfire before we ended the trek the scouts discussed their experiences and collectively said, "Wouldn't it be great if our less advantaged friends could have had this experience."

Chapter Twenty one The Boy Scouts of America

As we traveled on the trail, we picked up any trash we encountered. The rules of a good camper is that he should pickup anything in the forest that the Lord did not put there. This was consistent with our training. We made a stretcher with two poles and a blanket and all of the trash we had found was put on the stretcher. One of the scouts placed two boots which stuck out from under the blanket. The stretcher was carried into Bell Meadow and the awaiting parents thought we were bringing back a casualty with us. Their concern turned into laughter when they realized it was only trash we had picked up on the trek.

They provided us with sandwiches and fresh fruit which we were very glad to get.

At a meeting of all the participants in my home a week later where I presented each one with a certificate of accomplishment of their recent survival trek. We discussed the recommendation made at the last campfire. We decided that next summer we would arrange for a three day outing for developmentally handicapped young people in "Tuolumne County to share some of our experiences."

The candidates for the next trek were selected by the County Social Services Agency. Our next trek scheduled for the following summer would be to Spicer Lake. The first phase would be by canoe for three miles up to Spicer Lake where they would arrive to a landing point within a mile from the designated campsite. There they would sleep for two nights in a camping environment.

In 1985, we purchased a large King of the Road trailer and went south through Baja, California stopping at

Guerero Negro and spent overnight on the beach. This was the annual spawning area for the gray whale. In the early morning we could watch the big gray whales that had come down from Alaska giving birth to their young 50 to 100 yards offshore. This was a very rewarding experience; Sheila and I felt very privileged at the opportunity of being so close to these large mammals. We proceeded south through Muleje and Loreto and on to Cabo San Lucas. I went fishing on a boat out of Loreto and caught my first sail fish! It was the first time I had been so lucky.

In 1986 my brother Richard and his wife Mary visited us at Mi-Wuk, California and went with us on our trip south and east. We stopped in San Diego and met for the first time with my cousin, Marilyn, who had been the News Anchor at the KGO-Radio Station of San Diego.

After 10 days in San Diego we traveled east on Highway 8 and shortly after crossing the border into Arizona, noticed a sign of a nearby town called Hyder and took time to visit. There were only a few old buildings still located there. We visited the only saloon still operating and asked the bartender, "How did it get its name?" He asked, "Why the interest since it was known as a ghost town!" We introduced ourselves and he said it was named after two Lebanese attorneys named Hyder from Phoenix who visited the nearby volcanic hot springs for their health and felt much rejuvenated after their visit speaking highly about the therapeutic waters. These two men were uncles of Marilyn.

Two nearby gentlemen from the railroad company overheard their comments and since the nearby rail junction had never been named, they said, "This junction

Chapter Twenty one The Boy Scouts of America

will be named Hyder."

We then proceeded east stopping at El Paso, Texas and visited our cousins who had a large clothing manufacturing company. Their company had more than 4,000 employees most of whom were Mexicans. The trade name of their clothing was "Farrah" - jeans, suits, and dresses.

We stopped at Mobile, Alabama, then south to Bonita Springs, Florida where Dick and Mary had a condo. We spent a week visiting friends there. Then we went up the east coast, visited my cousin Marie at Alexandria, Virginia, our friends Ned and Bernadette Day who live in the Shenandoah National Forest and the Doyles, at Williamsburg, Virginia. We spent a few days there and proceeded to Connecticut and stopped for a week at the home of my brother Dick and his wife Mary, at Branford.

We then went up through Niagara Falls, crossed into Canada and stopped at a recreational vehicle (RV) park on Mantoulian Island where Sheila and I spent two days playing golf.

We then proceeded west through Canada, south through Minnesota on to Kansas City, Kansas to visit Sheila's relatives, Arthur and Marlene Bunker and Mr. and Mrs. Manti Maverick. We went west of Kansas City on Highway 40 and stopped at Russell, Kansas where my trailer, the King of the Road (KOR) was built. We took this opportunity to get some warranty items repaired and a deep freezer installed in the trailer.

This was also the home of Presidential hopeful Robert Dole. Sheila and I enjoyed a wonderful steak dinner at Russell which seemed to have the most tender steaks we ever had. The restaurateur told us where the steaks could be obtained in Russell at wholesale. We purchased 25 pounds of top sirloin steaks which we would carry home in our new deep freezer. We stopped at Denver, Colorado to visit Sheila's niece, Debby Cook-Kelley and husband Bryan who was a detective in the Denver Police Department. Bryan also owned a small cattle ranch just east of Denver. Debbie is the daughter of Sheila's sister, Anne Cook. Then we headed back to our home at Mi-Wuk Village, California.

In 1991 I was in contact with an organization called Boats U.S. of which I was a member. The group was planning for a visit to Athens, Greece and Istanbul, Turkey. The plan called for members to charter sailing boats to visit the Greek Islands. I chartered a 51-foot sloop which contained four separate staterooms. Each of these contained separate bathrooms with accompanying facilities. Bill and Lillian Ferris agreed to join us along with another couple from New Orleans, Louisiana. One of the staterooms remained empty since Boat U.S. said no one else was interested.

I also requested at the time of the charter for the coordinator at Athens, Greece to employ a Greek boat boy at our expense who knew the Greek Islands to join us as a crew member. His name was Jimmy; he was a very handsome 22-year-old with a typical Grecian profile which the ladies enjoyed. We spent 10 days sailing through the islands as a flotilla stopping at a different port every afternoon and stayed overnight. We went ashore every afternoon to a recommended restaurant to party and enjoy the local Greek cuisine. The islands were beautiful and the turquoise water was so clear you could see more

Chapter Twenty one The Boy Scouts of America

than 30 feet down to the sand and fish below.

The sailing trip ended at Athens, Greece where we turned in our boats. In the late afternoon our group flew to Istanbul where we spent three days visiting the many wonders of that ancient city. At that point of our journey our group broke up and we went our separate ways.

Bill, Lillian, Sheila, and I flew on to Cairo, Egypt to visit friends and relatives there. A week later we returned to our homes in the United States.

In 1994, Bill Ferris who was now a United States Navy Captain, retired, paid us a visit and related his recent experience of having made an RV trip with his brother-in-law and grandchildren up to Anchorage, Alaska and return.. He said on the way back from the Yukon they had a flat tire and did not have the equipment to make the repair. An Alaskan highway repair vehicle came by and offered assistance. They said they would have to tow them to a nearby town where the necessary repairs would have to be done. They were told the repairs could take two days to be completed. They went into the town to a recommended restaurant and had a delicious seafood dinner. They were told the town was called Hyder.

Due to the magnitude of ships and prospective gold miners arriving at Stewart the building of piers expanded rapidly two miles to the west of Stewart to Alaskan territory. As a result the border between Canada and Alaska bisected Stewart and the portion to the west of the International border became known as Hyder, Alaska.

The citizens of Hyder and Stewart overcame their various community needs in a most wonderful co-acceptance of community development. The Canadian

Mounties provided Stewart and Hyder with police protection inasmuch as Hyder had no police department. Hyder had no schools so children went to school in Stewart. Stewart had no post office so they used the one in Hyder. The area bordering on Hyder to the north including the Salmon River constituted a protected grizzly bear preserve. As a result, the United States Department of Agriculture established a protected grizzly bear research station and park for study of the habitat species.

A person at a nearby table at the restaurant said she was the President of Hyder Chamber of Commerce and welcomed them to Hyder. Bill went on to say his dear friend was also named Hyder. The President of the Chamber of Commerce said they were planning a 100-year anniversary celebration in 1995 and would like to extend an invitation to Mr. Hyder. They also wanted to inquire whether the person that Bill talked about could have been a relative of the person the town was named after. Bill told them when he got back to California he would investigate and let the President of the Chamber know what he found out. When he returned to California he told me in detail what had transpired on his trip to Alaska. We did some inquiries and found out that the engineer who had performed the services at Hyder had been born in Lawrence, Massachusetts of Lebanese parents and was a relative. He received his engineering degree in Montreal, Canada.

The Canadian government became concerned about the large number of Yukon gold rush miners arriving in Stewart, British Columbia. The facilities there were determined inadequate and the government decided to

Chapter Twenty one The Boy Scouts of America

send an engineer to establish more adequate facilities. The population of Stewart had risen sharply from 300 to 5,000 persons within weeks. Stewart was the most southwestern point of Canada at the end of a misty fjord and was 100 miles inland from the Pacific Ocean surrounded by glaciers. The business-minded sea captains at Seattle, Washington would advertise that they could take prospective miners north and 100 miles east and closer to the Yukon; they had many takers.

In 1995 Sheila, Craig, and I went north with our King of the Road trailer attached to a one ton-4-wheel drive truck. We were accompanied by Captain Ferris and his grandsons Ephraim and Micah in their own RV rig. The RV Park where we stayed was in Stewart. When we walked down the road in Hyder word had already spread that Maurice Hyder had arrived. We were stopped constantly by Hyder residents who wanted to see my driver's license to be sure I was a Hyder. We satisfied their curiosity.

On the third day after we had arrived, my son Mark, his wife Susan and Bill's son, Michael arrived at Hyder by float plane where we picked them up and took them to the RV site.

The next day we had made arrangements with a local fishing guide to fish the Misty Fjord. We left early in the morning in the guide's boat and powered out to the center of the fjord where a 9-foot square floating raft was anchored. The guide took a 2-burner Coleman stove and put it on the raft. Then he took a 24x24 in large stainless steel open container, filled it half full of water from the fjord and put it on the stove, covered it and the stove on low. Our also guide dropped a 3-foot diameter rebar steel covered with chicken wire which had many fish heads and fish carcasses attached. He dropped it to the bottom of the fjord.

We then got back on the boat trolling the fjord for salmon. We fished four hours and caught a few small fish but no salmon.

Our guide returned us to the float about 12 noon and we tied up along side. He then turned the Coleman stove on high to bring it to a boiling point. He also threw herbs he had brought with him into the pot including salt and pepper. The guide then retrieved with the screen with the help0 of the crew, which was loaded with more than 200 Dungness crabs. He inspected his catch throwing the males into the pot and throwing the females back overboard.

The women stayed at the RV Park. Bill, his son Michael, and grandsons Ephram and Micah, Mark, Craig, and I enjoyed a two hour fabulous crab luncheon. The guide brought a large jar of cocktail sauce. After lunch we again prepared the wire screen and dropped it in the fjord.

We then left for the Salmon River which emptied into the fjord and there our fishing for salmon was fantastic. We would cast into the stream and hook 30-40 pound salmon to our hearts' content. After salmon fishing we stopped at the raft, pulled up the screen with more crab than before putting the males in an ice cooler, returning to Hyder and the RV Park.

On the way to the RV Park we stopped at a restaurant and gave all the crab to the owner who said he would cook 30 of the crab which we would pick up later for our dinner that evening. We spent the next day observing the giant grizzly bears and their cubs frolicking around them. We also enjoyed watching the bears grabbing salmon going up the river reaching out with their big right paw and grabbing a salmon. They would take two big bites out of a salmon tossing the rest of the carcasses aside.

We were then presented with dozens of bald eagles and ospreys who fed on the carcasses of the salmon. This is where Mark almost got into deep trouble. He spotted a big mother grizzly playing with her cubs at the edge of the river when he decided to video tape them but the grizzly mother objected to being photographed and took off after Mark who ran like hell! We called to a nearby forest ranger that quickly intervened getting between Mark and the bear, and pointed pepper spray at the grizzly. The grizzly bear quickly put on the brakes, stopped, turned, walking away with the cubs following. This was the end of another perfect day.

Chapter Twenty Two
The Departure

CHAPTER TWENTY TWO THE DEPARTURE

The next day Mark, Susan, and Michael were picked up by the float plane and returned to the United States via Ketchikan, Alaska. Two days later we packed up our rigs and headed for home.

The approximate year round population of Hyder was 175.

In 1996 it was reduced by one person who had ended up in the belly of a grizzly bear!

In February 1996 I was notified by the President of the Chamber of Commerce of Hyder that the main building that had contained their library had burned to the ground. She said they had lost their books and would have difficulty replacing them.

I responded that I would help them by sending them my extensive library at Mi-Wuk. This consisted to more the 3,500 hard cover books that included and Encyclopedia Britannica. The shipment would also include more than

1,000 paper back fiction books. This was my gift to Hyder, Alaska.

In the spring of 1995 Sheila and I traded in our King of the Road trailer and purchased a Fleetwood Discovery 40-foot motor home. The salesman who sold the new Discovery to us was our son, Mark, who had extorted the virtues of this new RV that had come on the market. Mark was a salesman at the Chico Fleetwood Sales Department. As a result thereof Sheila and I sat with Mark and customized the rig; Sheila selected the drapes, blinds and interiors. It had two air conditioners, three TVs, and a top mounted automatic satellite cable receiver.

In March 1999 we took our usual trip south to San Diego, and then went east re-discovering all the history along Route 66.

After crossing the Mississippi we went south to Alabama and Florida visiting my brother Richard and his wife Mary at Bonita Springs, Florida.

Then we went up the east coast visiting my cousin Marie and the Doyles in Virginia and relatives in Connecticut and Massachusetts. Then we headed for Niagara Falls. We went north into Canada, then west. We entered the United States through Minnesota to Kansas City, again visiting Arthur and Marlene Bunker.

After a fine time there we headed west on U.S. 40 through Denver and Highway 50 back to Mi-Wuk. We had a great Christmas in December 1999 with all our family.

After dinner on 8 April 2001 I was working in my office finalizing and paying some bills when Sheila stopped at the door of my office on her way to bed. She asked me how

Chapter Twenty Two The Departure

much longer I would be. I said, "I have two more checks to write and I'll follow you in two minutes." I finished my work, got up two minutes later and headed for bed.

As I stepped from my office and turned right I saw Sheila lying on the carpet six feet away and rushed to her. I checked her throat pulse but nothing seemed to be working. When she fell, her head had hit the big concrete planter in the hallway and had opened up the flesh so I could see the white of her skull as I was giving her CPR.

I reached for my cell phone in my pocket, dialed 911, and explained my difficulty continuing my CPR awaiting the ambulance. It was snowing outside and there was more than six inches on the ground.

The ambulance that was stationed at Twain Harte only five minutes away, took 30 minutes to reach me.

The medic team whom I knew personally rushed inside and Marty Rosebaum, the EMT, tapped me on the shoulder and said, "She's gone. Let us take over."

They tried to revive her with electronic paddles but were unsuccessful.

The coroner was called and they picked up Sheila on a gurney and put her in the ambulance and said, "Under the circumstances of her death, an autopsy will have to be performed."

I called my children to notify them of our loss.

My partner and companion had left me. When Sheila passed, the following is a message I sent to all of our friends and relatives.

(continued in the next chapter)

Chapter Twenty Three
Sheila's Message

Chapter Twenty Three Sheila's Message

Don't grieve for me, for now I'm free,
I'm following the path God laid for me.
I took His hand when I heard Him call,
I turned my back and left it all.
I could not stay another day
To laugh, to love, to work or play.
Tasks left undone must stay that way,
I found that peace at the close of day.
If my parting has left a void,
Then fill it with remembered joy.
A friendship shared, a laugh, a kiss;
Oh yes, these things I too will mss.
Be not burdened with times of sorrow;
I wish you the sunshine of tomorrow,
My life's been full, I savored much,
Good friends, good times,
A loved one's touch.
Perhaps my time seemed all too brief;
Don't lengthen it now with undue grief.
Lift up your heart and share with me;
God wanted me now; He set me free.

Sheila Howard Hyder
October 25, 1934 – April 8, 2001

Sheila Howard Hyder, 66, of Mi Wuk Village died Sunday at her home.

Mrs. Hyder was born in Hong Kong. She graduated from Sacred Heart Academy in Palo Alto, Rollins College of Orlando , Fla., and received a bachelor of science degree (B.S.) at American College in Beirut, Lebanon.

She married Maurice Hyder in December 1957 and with him traveled extensively around the world. Mr Hyder worked for the U.S. Department of State and traveled to embassies all over the world.

Their three children all were born in different countries- Benghazi, Libya; Beirut Lebanon; and Kabul, Afghanistan. And the family was once approached by Garry Moore of the "I've Got a Secret" television show, who was interested in the family of five Americans who were all born in different countries.

Mrs. Hyder was an active member and past- president of All Saints Catholic Church Ladies guild, and was active with the Golden Heritage of Boy Scouts and the Tuolumne General Hospital Ladies Auxiliary.

Chapter Twenty Three Sheila's Message

In addition to her husband, she is survived by her children, Mark Hyder of Chico , Ca. ,Craig Hyder od Bayport, N.Y. and Sharon Hyder of Rohnert Park, Ca. and six grand children, Elizabeth and Emily Hyder, both of Chico, and Jamie, Drew, Mark, and Sean Hyder. Al of Bayport.

A memorial service will be held Wednesday at 11a.m. at Heuton Memorial Chapel in Sonora. A reception will be held after the service at the Steinmetz House, 116 W. Bradford Ave. Sonora.

The family requests , in lieu of flowers, remembrances be made to the Aahmes Shrine Center , 170 Lindbergh Ave, Livermore, Ca. 94550.

Sheila Howard Hyder

Epilogue

Epilogue

Sheila became my wife, constant companion, and my partner for life n which we shared 44 great years of marriage. Sheila was born in Hong Kong, China on 25 October 1934. Together we sired three children, Mark born n Benghazi, Libya, Craig in Beirut, Lebanon, and Sharon born in Kabul, Afghanistan.

Sheila graduated from Rollins University at Orlando, Florida. She was a little over 6 feet tall in her stocking feet and a natural athlete at Rollins. She received 3 silver cups in recognition of her ability. She was the top volleyball player, top basketball player, ad softball player where she held down the first base position. Sheila was also the author of a publication of original children's stories which was published in November 2014, and is available at Amazon and the American Library of Congress.

During our early years together we loved to go hiking in the back country of many countries where I served. On one such occasion while we ere hiking 10 miles into the mountains of Afghanistan, she slipped and fell off the trail breaking her left forearm.

Since we were very far from any help, I told her I would try to reset her arm since I had studied first aid. I told her it would be painful and what should I do? She said go ahead.

I had no pain killer but gave her 3 aspirin from my medical kit and proceeded to reset the bone, padded, and splinted her arm and arranged for a sling to keep it immobilized. We continued our hike back to Kabul where she received x-rays and examination of the break. The surgeon said everything was done correctly and he could not improve on it and she'd be able to use her arm in about 4 weeks. This is one example of the gutsy woman I married.

In our early years someone had tipped off Gary Moore of the television show, "I've Got a Secret." He tried for five years to get us on his show because of our unusual circumstances. My consistent movement on assignments precluded our appearance on his program. Our secret was that our family was all Americans at birth, born in five different countries and in accordance with the rules of the United States Constitution, met the conditions where any one of us could run for President of the United States.

In 1956, Maurice Hyder was approached by the United States State Department and offered a direct appointment into the Foreign Service. He accepted the appointment and joined the department in 1956. He traveled the world in interesting and challenging situations. He retired from the State Department in November 1977. He looked forward to a well-deserved relaxing future. But this was not to be!

Because of his special qualifications, two days after his retirement he was contacted by the State Department to undertake a mission in the Middle East. He was hired under a special contract by a corporation chartered in North Carolina

Epilogue

conducting specialized types of procurement requested by the Executive Branch of the United States Government. This was the beginning of many short-term TDYs around the world until Sheila, in 1989, called the State Department and said, "Enough is enough. I want my husband at home," and that ended my direct service to the United States State Department.

All Mr. Hyder could say when asked, that it was a very interesting and challenging life he led and he was looking forward to spend the rest of his life in the arms of his bride.

The Vital Statistics of Maurice J. Hyder

I am a member of the American Legion, Post #0681 at Twain Harte, California. My dues paid up in full.

I am a member of the Veterans of Foreign Affairs, paid in full at Oroville, California.

I am a Master Mason and my home lodge is St. Paul #14, Newport, Rhode Island.

I am a member of the Scottish Rites Mason, Valley of Stockton.

I am retired President of the Mother Lode Shrine Club, 1968-1972.

I am scheduled to receive my75th recognition as a Master Mason in June, 1918.

I received my Honorable Discharge from the United States Navy, 1939-1947; I was separated at Pensacola, Florida in 1947.

I am a BSA Wood badge 4-bead Course Director.

ACKNOWLEDGEMENTS

Acknowledgements

I would like to thank those who helped me in the preparation and completion of this book. I particularly wish to thank Bonnie Bryan, Paradise, California, Tom Watson, Paradise, California, Maureen (Mo) Garcia, Chico, California, and Captain William Ferris, United States Navy (Ret.), Mark Hyder, Chico, California.

My Most Sincere Thanks

Maurice Hyder

www.ingramcontent.com/pod-product-compliance
Lightning Source LLC
Chambersburg PA
CBHW060822050426
42453CB00008B/539